CERTIFIABLY BULIMIC

by

Susan L. Merkel

d p
DISTINCTIVE PUBLISHING CORP.

Distinctive Publishing Corporation
P.O. Box 17868
Plantation, FL 33318-7868
Copyright ©1992 by Susan L. Merkel
All rights reserved.
Printed in the United States of America
Price: $12.95

Library of Congress Cataloging-in-Publication Data

Merkel, Susan L., 1947-
    Certifiably bulimic / Susan L. Merkel.
        p.   cm.
    ISBN 0-942963-15-6 : $12.95
    1. Merkel, Susan L., 1947- . 2. Bulimia—Patients—United
States—Biography. 3. Depressed persons—Patients—United
States—Biography. 4. Alcoholics—United States—Biography. I. Title.
    RC552.B84A3   1991
    616.85'263'0092—dc20
    [B]   91-14993
                                                                              CIP

TABLE OF CONTENTS

INTRODUCTION AND DEDICATION

This book is not written for any monetary reward. Nor is it written to blame or malign anyone. It is written in the hope that someone else's journey into healing can be a little less painful and lonely. I wasn't going to write my story until I had achieved total abstinence from my bulimia, but honestly speaking, that goal may be another year or two down the road. Besides, I now accept that progress, for me, cannot be measured by a reduction in the number of times I binge and purge. Progress at this point in my life is an increase in the number of present moments that I rejoice in being alive . . . that I am filled with gratitude for each and every gift I see, touch, feel, taste, and hear.

The key to my unfolding was embracing the concept of the Inner Child. Once my inner child, Little Suzy, and I established a trusting bond, my depressed, deprived, and fearful personality began peeling away like old paint. Sometimes huge chunks fell off while other times only a thin veneer slipped away. My move from an isolated, dungeon-like existence into the Light has been both excruciating and jubilant.

I believe that I am alive today because of the tenacity and the brilliant beauty of my soul, which has directed every scene I have starred in during this lifetime. And I find that this original essence that I am bubbles within Little Suzy.

She is laughter, dance, song, and love. She, unlike the other aspects of my personality, is imbued with the Lifeforce which kept my dead shell from bashing itself on the reef and crumbling into a million pieces. So it is that I dedicate my book to her. For among all the loving, supportive people and spirits who have guided me, it was she who unlocked the door. Thank you, Little Suzy!

"Love is what heals the personality.
Love is the energy of the soul."

The Seat Of The Soul by Gary Zukav

1

The Trauma

I WAS BORN OCTOBER 30, 1947, in Oklahoma, and I "died" July 23, 1950. My parents said they were delighted with the arrival of their second daughter and their third child. I had an older sister, Joan, who was eight years of age, and an older brother, Joe Ben, who was five years old. For Mother, the birth was an easy one, and for Daddy, I was a squirming, real live birthday present. So, not only did he and I share the same astrological sign, but the identical day of birth. Throughout my life, this fateful occurrence would bring me tremendous pride and wonderment.

After my first week on earth, I adjusted to life and began accepting formula. Because I spit up all nourishment in those first few days, Mother and Daddy phoned a pediatrician friend in California, asking his advice. He immediately flew to Oklahoma to investigate. The general conclusion was that I was suffering from colic and with the passage of time I would settle down and things would be normal. On the surface this was a valid assumption.

Joe Ben loved me very much. He would play with me and drag his friends over to see me. I developed a bond with him which was equally as strong. My father's medical practice was thriving, and he continued to amass ranch land in the county south of where we lived. My mother anchored the home and managed the household. Our family was like other post-World War II families in that life seemed hopeful and chances for prosperity were within grasp. Catastrophe was the last thing on anyone's mind. Yet on the morning of July 23, 1950, my family crashed from a fairly functional unit to a bleeding, dismembered carcass. Shattered were any joy or dreams that we were savoring, individually or collectively.

The spring of 1950 around my hometown had been a very wet one. Even by the middle of the summer, creeks, ponds, and lakes were brimming with water. Some of the creeks, in fact, were raging torrents with dangerous eddies. The creek which would flood low-lying areas of my daddy's ranch after drenching rains was in such a state. Nevertheless, on the morning of July 23, my sister Joan, Joe Ben, and one of his best friends climbed into the ranch foreman's vehicle for an outing in the country. Daddy had patients to tend and could not join the adventurers. Mother agreed with Daddy's decision to let the children go. This mutual decision would tear them apart for the rest of their lives.

The main entrance to the ranch was impassable due to the flood waters, so the foreman parked his vehicle beside the swollen creek and got out to survey his predicament. He instructed the youngsters to remain inside the car and not to venture out. The boys finally got permission to get out of the car and walk around, but with warnings to stay away from the creek. They ambled over to an area behind some trees and out of sight of the automobile. They spied a brief span of water between them and a bridge and judged it to be shallow. They reasoned that if they could wade to the bridge, they would have discovered an entry to the ranch.

Joe Ben decided to cross first. A stick was broken to use for support and to feel the bottom of the creek as he forded it. After two steps Joe Ben lost his footing and tumbled. His companion instantly grabbed another stick and shoved it toward Joe Ben. It was only inches short. The forceful current began sucking Joe Ben away and as his friend tried to reach him, he, too, pitched forward into the creek. The little friend screamed for the foreman, who came running. The man dived into the main current to rescue Joe Ben while Joe Ben's pal found a log on the bank and crawled to safety. After what felt like an eternity to the terrified little friend, the foreman emerged from the wild water with Joe Ben in his arms. He and the children raced back into town.

During the return trip, Joan attempted artificial respiration on Joe Ben's limp body. Once rendezvoused with Daddy, Joe Ben was rushed to a hospital. All efforts to revive him failed. My father was never the same again. For that matter, neither were the rest of the family.

The philosophy in those days was to grieve at the funeral and then to bury one's pain and march forward with a stiff upper lip. There were no support groups, and professional help was considered only for the mentally unbalanced. Consequently, each of us in my family retreated into his or her own mental corner; we coped as best we could inside our own isolated prisons.

Daddy neglected his practice and received solace from alcohol. He was drunk for six weeks. Mother was drained because she now not only had her own ever present torment, but two needy daughters and a suicidal husband.

I am an extremely sensitive person, and even at two-and-a-half years old, I could feel the unspoken chaos around me. My terror of abandonment and not being able to survive coupled with my confusion about Joe Ben's whereabouts (a two-and-a-half-year-old views death as reversible) propelled me into rage. My young psyche was reeling. I was helpless and powerless. Instead of releasing these emotions, though, I decided, however a two-and-a-half-year-old mentality does, that I would repress all memory and all feeling associated with this loss. I also knew, somewhere deep inside me, that from now on I had to take care of myself. There was nobody there to help me. I had to go it alone — depending on no one, **especially** men! It would not be until age 18 that I reconnected with this damaged child and felt her raw and monumental pain.

2

Childhood

MEMORIES FROM AGES THREE TO ELEVEN are a fairly large black hole. Though I didn't realize it, those first few years after Joe Ben's death I was fueling a subliminal core pool of potent emotions which would erupt in later years as very destructive behavior patterns. As a defense mechanism, I still only remember selective, carefree episodes, and until June, 1987, I nonchalantly minimized the vague aura of gloom and suffocation. This process kept me from unraveling.

The real drama was proceeding in my unconscious. My depression increased as I became the mirror for my parents' depression while also grieving the loss of my sense of my True Self. I received a minimum amount of validation to keep my True Self fighting, but not enough to let it fly free.

Feeling another child "would help," one year and two weeks after Joe Ben's death, on August 6, 1951, my mother gave birth to a third daughter, christened Carol. I interpreted this baby as a message to me that I had failed in restoring happiness to my family. Since I had obviously not done my job, they had cast me aside and introduced another girl-child who might do what I had failed in doing. I felt worthless, abandoned a second time, and furious! I felt my parents must not have loved and valued me, so I made a decision. I would lean on myself. I would solve everything on my own and I would not bother anyone! Furthermore, I would "become" a boy. Surely if I could just be tough enough, smart enough, and independent enough, my parents' son could be replaced, their happiness restored, and they would love me again. This poor, needy child thus closed herself up and off.

Still, if I had to choose a period of my life that I would recall as "happy," this era would be my choice. Ordinary little girl activities occupied my days. Brownies, Girl Scouts, dancing, piano and voice lessons, playing "house" as well as Cowboys and Indians, and attending birthday parties were all marvelous fun.

Summertime was the best time of all! I could be outside most of the day, and anytime I was outside I felt safe, free, and giggly.

The two neighbor boys, my little sister Carol, and I formed a tight relationship involving lots of feuds and lots of sharing. We would be "blood brothers" at ten o'clock in the morning, and by one o'clock in the afternoon we were screaming insults at each other through the twelve-foot hedge separating our homes.

Running around barefooted was rapture, and how brave we were catching lightning bugs in the evening darkness or toads near the garage light.

What voyagers we became when we ambled three blocks to the neighborhood mom-and-pop grocery store after our naps to buy ice cream or a candy bar!

School months were the opposite. I was filled with dread that I would not please my teachers and preoccupied with the idea that my peers did not like me. In fact, I developed a fear of everything. What if some stranger kidnapped me while I was walking to or from school? What if my house and family were gone when I came home from school one day? Was my daddy going to kill me? Was the older kid down the street going to chop off my head and flush it down the toilet like he threatened to do? I didn't really know and I felt terribly susceptible to harm. All I knew was that I couldn't talk about it and I had to act brave and happy.

I elevated my daddy to a pedestal, and I enmeshed with my mother. Whenever I tried to separate, either through a temper tantrum or an expression of an original idea or project, my fear, guilt, and shame reached such overpowering proportions that I cowered back into myself. My sense of betrayal was intolerable, and I desperately needed their love, so I demurred to the obedient, quiet, respectful model I knew would warrant their approval.

My parents were living a mental hell, and I was constantly aware of their suffering. But it was Daddy, whose underlying rage felt tangible to me, that made me walk the line. I worshipped him while simultaneously quaking in his presence.

One evening when I was about six or seven, he whipped me for some trivial rambunctiousness I can't now recall. He sat on the edge of the bathtub; I draped myself belly down over his knees, and he slapped my bare bottom repeatedly. His savageness terrified and confounded me. What had I done to deserve such wrathful punishment? I must be a totally evil person! It goes without saying I went out of my way thereafter never to cross him.

Physically, I was growing up strong and healthy. I recovered from the various childhood illnesses intact. Until fourth grade I ate whatever was on my plate and enjoyed it. There was no yearning for more. By the fourth grade I was really tasting food and really relishing every bite. Sweets were coveted, and I always wanted more of them, though I didn't get seconds. I was aware of hunger feelings, and I was aware of satisfying those hunger pangs. I ate. I negated hunger. It was simple. Sometimes I puzzled over why other children complained about Spam or navy beans and corn bread served in the school lunchroom. We certainly had it better than the starving children in China! Only when Mother bought me clothes was I concerned with my physical appearance, and even then it was not in a fat/thin context.

Shortly after turning eleven (sixth grade), a slight uneasiness began creeping into my consciousness. Of course, I couldn't articulate my apprehensions, but a life-changing milestone, menstruation, was approaching! I would cross the threshold into womanhood and leave my childhood behind forever.

There was something else I was terrified of losing, but I didn't know what. I tried to pluck out and name the nebulous anxiety, but every attempt to search my brain was abruptly cut off. Instead of directing this poison arrow of fear and anger and confusion outward, I deflected it back into myself. I actively and consciously began my self-abuse with my undershirt ritual.

One item of underwear my mother decided I needed to wear was an undershirt. Not the plain, sleeveless design like men wear, but something more feminine — something with simple eyeletting around the scooped neck and straps. They were very pretty and I wouldn't object to wearing one now, but at age eleven I balked. That is, until I discovered what an excellent flattening device they made.

I knew I couldn't stop Nature's plan for my maturation, but I could surely hide the early developments. I would not go into femininity without a fight! I stretched the undershirt as tightly as I could down to my waist. On the inside of my garment's waistband I safety pinned the left side of the undershirt to the garment and the right side of the undershirt to the garment. Voila! I was still a child.

Sadly, I would remain imprisoned within that child, not having any inkling about how to escape. My only recourse was to increase the self-torture during my twelfth year and my subsequent teenage years.

3

Teenage Years

JUNIOR HIGH SCHOOL! Was I thrilled! My twelfth year (seventh grade) was a huge paradox. I wanted to be a sophisticated young lady and wear a bra, lipstick, high heels, and hose. Yet tugging at the hem of my new seventh grade wardrobe was my neglected Inner Child.

I was proud as a peacock of our new country home but strangely embarrassed by its opulence. The family had shrunk because my older sister graduated from high school and married in 1957. I do not remember a ceremony for either occasion. It was like Joan evaporated, and the four of us remaining seemed to be more remote than ever.

Not surprisingly, I didn't enlarge my circle of friends. I stayed close to the companions I had in grade school. I did develop a crush on a boy who would be the love of my life until I married, but I doubt if he ever knew of my deep affection for him.

Studying took up more of my time, and good grades became an obsession. I was not yet pushing for straight "A's," but a "C" on my report card made me feel like a complete failure. School was drudgery and I could hardly wait until 3:35 p.m., when classes were dismissed. Mother picked Carol and me up every afternoon, drove us home, and I began studying anew. No way was I hanging around for extracurricular activities.

A total bookworm I wasn't, though. On weekdays, when homework assignments were light, and on weekends, I allowed myself romping space. Bike riding, softball batting practice with Carol, walking with the dogs (we always had a dog or two), tether ball, swimming, sledding in winter when it snowed, exploring at the ranch on Saturday afternoons, and dolls were options.

Another clue to my internal distress, though I was oblivious to it, was my ritual doll playing. I was not "playing dolls" where I was the gentle, nurturing mother. I was staging a play. Identical dolls were used for the characters, and the plot was always re-enacted with the same ending. The overtones felt darkly sinister, so I conducted my plays behind my closed bedroom door, and if anyone knocked on my door, I surreptitiously flung the dolls under my bed. From there they were not visible because my bedspread touched the floor. At the time, I could not understand why the groom doll (who in my imagination became a brave, mighty Cowboy) shyly approached his demure, coquettish bride doll (who in my imagination became the impeccable schoolmarm) and after polite conversation, began kissing and touching her in her private places even though she objected. He always raped her, though in my twelve-year-old mind, I wasn't clear about what rape really was. I was incredibly naive or else couldn't tolerate the thought. In retrospect, I understand that this rape fantasy allowed me to deal with the unmentionable topic of sex.

A bonus upon entering junior high school was the extensive cafeteria line. Now I had three different choices for an entree as well as for vegetables and dessert. I thought this system was classy, and I took advantage of all the tasty items. My favorites were the chicken fried steak, mashed potatoes and white gravy, and the cinnamon apple crisp. This was the last year in my life that I ate without guilt and self-recrimination.

When my thirteenth birthday rolled around, I was ecstatic. Finally I was a teenager! It seemed endless in coming, but after a few months into it, I wanted to give it back. The inevitable happened, and I was devastated — sickened — when I saw that first stain of red on my underpants! I sobbed and cursed myself as if I were somehow defective for letting this happen. If it had not been for my home economics teacher taking class time to demonstrate how to pin on a Kotex pad (these were the days before adhesive pads), I would have been in the dark as to how to handle the situation. Whether my mother anticipated the big event or whether I asked her to buy a supply, there was a box of Kotex and a pile of newspaper sheets inside my bathroom cabinet awaiting my use.

For two years I actively battled with the assemblage of the pad onto the elastic belt. I hated the whole clumsy operation and persisted in believing there must be a more efficient way for women to wear these hygienic pads. Yes, I knew of the existence of tampons, but inserting a foreign object inside me was totally loathsome. The next best thing seemed to be an absorbency system built in the underwear itself. My version was a yard of toilet paper folded fanlike and laid inside the crotch of my panties. This invention was a miserable failure and only made me dishonor my femininity that much more.

Another fateful event marked my thirteenth year. My mother decided I should lose a little weight. She didn't put me on a restrictive diet, but cut down on food portions. I was a hefty eater, devouring two eggs, two strips of bacon, two slices of buttered toast with homemade jelly, and milk for breakfast. Lunch consisted of meat, two vegetables, dessert, and a carton of milk. A snack after school was available if I wanted it. Supper was always a full meal, often topped off with a slice of one of mother's incomparable pies. I felt extremely resentful when she altered my menu.

I began to look critically at my body and what I "saw" disgusted me. My first awareness of feeling "fat" started at this point. Now I was not only feeling ugly on the inside but on the outside as well. It was awful! I hated myself! Comparing myself to the other girls in my class became my pastime, and I never failed to come up on the short end of the stick. Self-deprecating thoughts zipped through my head like electricity. They were, for the moment, glancing blows. Knockout punches were not to assault me until I entered high school.

Starting in the ninth grade, I felt like I was placed into a vise grip. Everyone's grades were now compiled on a transcript which would be sent to any prospective colleges he/she might decide to enter. I somehow construed that one of the prestigious girls' schools back East should be my focus. That was fine with me. I had no use for boys anyway. I was going to be SOMEBODY, and a topnotch education would pave the way.

Consequently, I set my goal for straight "A's," put the blinders on, and charged unmercifully ahead. This tactic served me well for many years to come. I graduated from high school with a superb academic record but with a huge deficit in social skills.

Good grades were to be the only way I could get strokes from my parents, and they didn't seem to want to notice the terrible disintegration of my personality. Of course, I was a master of disguise and much of my despair was unleashed behind my closed bedroom and bathroom doors. The thought of open rebellion never occurred to me. I might be cast out . . . alone . . . How would I survive?

By tenth grade, all I thought I wanted was to graduate from high school with top honors, move out of the house, and start college.

My eating patterns became progressively distorted. My senior year I completely abolished breakfast and lunch. After school I was famished and to ease my dizzy spells, I binged on two or three bowls of canned peaches topped with cottage cheese. Sometimes I binged at supper, afterward feeling only a slight twinge of remorse for my lack of discipline.

Then again, I refused to sit at the supper table. Mother attributed my erratic behavior to "being a teenager" and rather than have an argument, left me alone. Occasionally, upstairs in my secluded room hearing the tinkle of silver-ware against china and the muffled voices of my family discussing events of their days, I put my head down upon my folded arms on my desk and cried. I wanted to be with them but I couldn't. I had to lose weight! (I weighed 120 pounds and was 5'3" tall. I would drop to 112 pounds by the end of the summer of 1965, yet I remained physically strong and healthy.)

Oddly, wicked persecution followed only ingestion of sweets, which were not out of proportion at this time. I believe this arose from my arbitrary rule that I did not deserve sweets unless I was an especially "good" girl. That implied doing everything perfectly. My strategy became one of snowballing deprivation. If I could disavow my feelings, I could disavow my needs. As is common in anorexia, of which I now had full-blown symptoms which were tossed off as stress, I felt increasingly superior and powerful in my own narrow, little world. People were going to notice me one day and say, "My, isn't she a perfect specimen — thin, intelligent, and self-sufficient!"

My thoughts became constantly malicious because I felt constantly imperfect. Vicious masochism eased those thoughts. When that internal voice demanded I beat myself, I did. I balled my fists and pummeled my abdomen, sobbing and chanting, "I hate you! I hate you! You are good for nothing! You ought to be dead! Why are you alive and Joe Ben dead? You are the one that should have died! You are no good!"

At times when I felt I deserved to endure real pain, I would bite into my forearms, drawing blood blisters. If that weren't enough, I slapped my legs with a doubled-up jump rope. This really hurt and always made me cry, unlike the other brutalities. I felt something inside me curl up and scream, as if I were injuring someone in there. I felt guilty about hurting it. To my punisher part, though, crying convinced me I had a long way to go to perfection. I was still very "weak."

My menstrual periods had stopped altogether by my junior year in high school. I was overjoyed that I didn't have to bother with the mess or the pain — or the reminder of my gender. In my senior year, Mother took me to a gynecologist who proclaimed I was just under a lot of stress trying to make good grades and waiting for the decision from Agnes Scott College in Decatur, Georgia, as to whether or not they would admit me. He assured us that time would balance everything out.

I had only three dates in high school. The first was with a buddy, and it really wasn't a date. He had broken up with his steady girl and needed someone to talk to. The second was in my junior year, and the boy treated me to a movie and a cherry tart topped with whipped cream afterward. He gave me my first kiss. I HATED it and swore I would never let another boy kiss me as long as I lived! My third date was to the Junior/Senior Prom when I was a junior. It was a lovely experience, and I thank the young man for making me feel so special. I don't believe he had a chance to kiss me because I fairly flew from his car into the house after the dance.

The heartbreak of my dating career is the fact that I was not invited to my Junior/Senior Prom as a senior. How desperately I wanted to go with the boy I had a crush on — or anyone, for that matter! That May evening of my Senior Prom I closed my bedroom door, as usual, opened one of my south-facing windows, knelt down beside it with my elbows propped on the sill, and I wept. I knew I was lonely. I knew I needed love and friends. I felt lost and hopeless. The blackness was overtaking me. Where was the fun and frolic that my classmates seemed to be enjoying? Why was such a worthless piece of humanity like me alive? I cried myself asleep that night trying to take comfort in my mother's advice, "Suzy, you're just a late bloomer."

4

The Crash

THE RAIN WAS POURING that mid-September day in
1965 at Dallas Love Field. It was a dark day in more than a
meteorological sense. I was flying to Atlanta, Georgia, to
embark on a whole new adventure. Something was wrong!
It didn't feel liberating like it did in my daydreams. It felt
terrifying! I didn't know if I really wanted to leave my family
now. There was safety with them, albeit precarious. But
plans were set and like Daddy firmly espoused, "If you start
something, finish it." Giving my family one last hug and kiss
and taking my seat on that plane was like going to the
guillotine. I kept prompting myself not to cry like a baby.

I didn't cry. The entire three or four weeks I was at Agnes
Scott College I did not cry. If only I had! If only I had opened
up to someone and expressed my fears. I did the "manly"
thing and held everything inside. Trouble was, I became
overtly depressed. I guess the college phoned my parents.
I don't remember. Anyway, Daddy drove over, withdrew
me from the college, and took me back home. He was very
kind, understanding and supportive.

I felt like a first-class failure! I was convinced I would
never make this black mark up to my daddy. I had failed in
fulfilling what I perceived as the ultimate "son" role: to
carry on the title "M.D.," Doctor of Medicine. I felt I was
not cut out to take up the reins of "doctor" like Daddy's

father, grandfather, and great-grandfather. Chalk up another victory for learned helplessness.

In January 1966, I went to live with my older sister, her husband, and their two small sons. I enrolled in the local college with great optimism. It wasn't long before those destructive thought patterns returned and persuaded me I was stupid and incompetent. I could not go home AGAIN with my tail between my legs. My parents would be humiliated and unable to hold their heads up in town ever again! All because of me, I believed.

There was only one option left. I tried to commit suicide by overdosing on tranquilizers. As I felt myself succumbing to the soft fuzziness of eternal sleep, I felt scared. I didn't want to die yet! I didn't want to live, but neither did I want to die.

My sister called my brother-in-law, and he rushed me to the hospital where I received emergency care. Then he put his arm around my shoulder and took me out to lunch. I will never forget the non-judgmental and loving treatment given to me by Joan and Jerry.

I was shipped home a second time. I got the attention I was unconsciously seeking from my parents. They must have been pretty shook up, although I remember no effusive greetings upon seeing them again.

The first indication I had that they were worried about me was when I learned that Daddy had selected a psychiatrist for me in Oklahoma City. I was relieved. Maybe a specialist could tell me what was wrong.

The next thing I knew, the psychiatrist, Daddy, and Mother had deemed it more beneficial (and certainly more economical) that I be an in-patient rather than a commuting out-patient. I was to be committed to the psychiatric ward of an Oklahoma City hospital. It was like somebody slammed me in the chest and knocked my breath away! The implications were horrendous. Every bad thought I had ever had about myself was confirmed, plus more! They all believed I was insane! That had to be it. Why was I the last to be privy to information about my case? Here I was, eighteen, being treated like a child again! I was raging inside. I felt betrayed, belittled, and unwanted. Yet I uttered not a word of objection, nor did I physically revolt.

I stayed in the hospital two weeks, and it was the most useless medical treatment I have ever experienced. The psychiatrist, pressed for time, held hasty sessions with me. In addition to these rounds, he ordered shock treatments. I couldn't understand why my parents had dumped me in this setting without a word of explanation. I was reeling with confusion.

When I came home, everyone acted as if nothing had happened. I spent most of my days behind my closed bedroom door. Whatever tiny bit of self-worth I possessed was shattered in the hospital. Life seemed a most cruel, miserable existence, and I was fed up with fighting. Severe depression engulfed me.

One day in late spring, out of pure desperation and driven by the instinct to survive, I phoned my aunt in Alabama and asked her if I could come spend the summer with her and her family. Mother and Daddy agreed to let me go.

Everyone else was still running my life, and I let them.

5

Young Adulthood and Marriage

IT WAS A CAREFREE SUMMER, that summer of 1966. I felt snug and loved in that tiny Alabama town of about 1,000 people. Everyone knew everyone else. Play and laughter were restored to my life. Preoccupation with my "fatness" disappeared. I ate anything and everything from Pop Tarts with apple jelly to peanut butter sandwiches. Food took its rightful place, that of bodily nourishment. By day I was assistant lifeguard at the local swimming pool, and by night I was either a participant or a bystander in a softball game. People were good to me, and I drenched myself in every ounce of their love. There was one handsome young man who particularly caught my eye and swept me off my feet. His name was Willie. He was to become my beloved husband two years later.

Summer eased into fall and I stayed on in Alabama. What I was going to do with my time was totally unclear. My aunt thought it would be beneficial if I enrolled in a small university thirty miles from our little town. I cringed. School again! Disgust was my initial reaction, but thrusting up from dormancy were my incessant sensations of inadequacy and timidity. My aunt would not be moved. With my insides screaming in fear and my outside expression flat, I passively agreed. But the day classes began, I passively rebelled.

My uncle found me on the bed, sluggish and sullen. I admitted I had downed a bottle or two of over-the-counter sleeping aids. He fetched my aunt who was quite perturbed with me. She gave me a lecture and then said we must agree not to tell anyone, especially Daddy, about this episode. It felt like someone kicked me in the stomach. My instincts were trying to warn me, but, of course, at that time trusting myself was unknown territory. I felt like a trapped animal with bars all around me. All my life I had been told to obey my elders for they knew best, so I blanked all doubts out of my head and mindlessly marched forward, trusting that one day something or someone in my external environment would deliver me to safety. I was still encased in the victim attitude. Once more I was operating as my two-and-a-half-year-old self.

My aunt and I concurred that I needed to prepare myself for the work force so that I could eventually find a job. Secretaries were in demand, so I enrolled at a vocational school thirty miles away.

In November, feeling wretched and homesick, I chucked all caution to the wind and wrote Daddy asking if I could come back to Oklahoma one last time. The sad thing was that I omitted expressing my feelings so that he would not think me a coward. He responded with the most honest, revealing letter I ever received from him. (I received very few letters from Daddy during his life, by the way.) He knew I had to break the apron strings and there was no gentle way of doing this. He had my best interests at heart when he wrote, "You will derive so much satisfaction and acquire much self-confidence when you set yourself up a challenge, fight for it, and conquer it. I, like you, have prayed — prayed often and for all of us and I know that the answers are good — but it will take a little time — all things worthwhile take a little time." Daddy had spoken. There was no use in arguing. At least he had been honest with me. So I thought.

Years after his death, when Mother and I were chatting one day and I told her how adrift I had felt during 1966, she began to cry. She explained that she and Daddy had disagreed vehemently about my fate. He wanted me to stay in Alabama, and she wanted me to return home. When I told her I had often felt guilty about living with my aunt and uncle and eating their food and using their house, Mother blinked incredulously. I had not been sponging off my relatives. Daddy had been paying them room and board from the beginning.

I felt like a piece of unwanted property.

I completed one year at the vocational school, found a job as a high school secretary, and married Willie on April 12, 1968. I was happier than I had ever been in my entire life! Someone truly loved me and wanted me! Everything was going to be okay now.

In truth, I was like many of my cohorts in this era — universally uninformed about what was involved in marriage. For instance, I had no idea marriage would trigger my unresolved childhood issues, sexuality being my powder keg. I had no idea how to confront, discuss, and compromise. To me problems were magically resolved by LOVE. I had no idea that I could argue, express anger, and expect to find my husband still loving me the next day. I had no idea that I was entitled to rights and needs, among them being the right to ask for what I wanted. I had no idea that I deserved respect. I had no idea that I could be a partner. I thought my role as wife relegated me to subservient status. I had no idea that couples had to work daily on their marriages to have successful ones. All I knew was the Snow White fairy tale where the handsome prince awakens the maiden with his kiss and they live happily ever after. In short, I had no idea who I was or what I could be. My identity was fashioned by my accomplishments, my titles, my possessions, and other people's validations.

I must have been very perplexing and frustrating to live with. On the other hand, considering the deficits I was working under, I did the best I knew how. I have never regretted my marriage to Willie and never will. He and his family were blessings in my life. I will always carry the parts of them they gave to me in my heart for the rest of my life. Had I waited to marry until I was the least bit knowledgeable about relationships, I wouldn't have married until age 42. I would have missed so much living and learning!

The first two years of married life were blissful, but by spring 1970, the fabric of our lives began to fray. I was restless and felt so worthless. I started withdrawing from people. In sharp contrast, Willie's banking career was skyrocketing, and he was involved in many civic projects.

In January of that year, in response to a 20-pound weight gain since my marriage, I had implemented a 1200-calorie per day diet that I found in a popular women's magazine. I stuck to it religiously. I didn't feel deprived . . . I thought.

Valentine's Day came and went and I was very sane about eating the chocolate candy Willie had given me. I was also exercising but not to excess. Then one day . . . I will never forget that spring afternoon as long as I live.

Midafternoon I was jolted with the most consuming need for sweets. In those days I baked quite a bit and enjoyed it. I pulled my favorite cookbook down from the shelf and found a recipe for "Lemon Pie Squares." It sounded super rich — just what I craved. My mouth watered the whole time I mixed ingredients and waiting until they came out of the oven seemed like an eternity. After they cooled a bit, I sectioned the 8x8 square pan and plucked two squares for my snack. The very first bite sent a shudder through my body. Something in my brain, like a miniature gun shot, fired. The sugary sweetness sent me flying, and I felt all my troubles float away. I wanted two more servings, then I'd stop. After that, just two more, and I would cover the pan and save the rest for Willie. BUT I COULD NOT STOP! I devoured the complete recipe.

Was I ever sick at my stomach! I raced into the bathroom and vomited. I cleaned up the splattered toilet and surrounding floor, washed my face, and glanced at the scale between the toilet and the sink. "I wonder if I gained any weight from these Lemon Pie Squares?" I pondered.

I hesitantly stepped on the scale and, lo and behold, I had gained nothing. I was holding my current weight of 113 pounds. This made me feel exhilarated!

"I think I have the ultimate way to lose weight. Wow! I wonder why no one has suggested this method before now? I don't ever have to worry about being fat again. I can eat anything I want and stay thin!" I chirped. I felt so free and so high. I was embracing a demon whose depravity I could never imagine.

That summer I completed three courses at a junior college — two "A's" and a "B." Overshadowing my pride was an indefinable oppression. Ever since classes started, I had experienced mild anxiety attacks which preceded and followed any academic stress. To relieve the gnawing agitation, I calmed myself with sweets. The craving for sweets became so urgent that many days I stopped at roadside groceries and bought donuts to tide me over until I got home. Sometimes I would throw up after overeating and sometimes I would not. By summer's end the uncomfortable, rapid pulsating which gripped my body began to increasingly generalize to petty frustrations. If a fuse was blown in the house, or a pencil lead broke while I was writing, I felt that anxiety swell.

By January 1971, I was bingeing and purging at least one time a week. By summer of 1971, I was bingeing and purging daily.

I was in agony. I didn't know what was happening to me. By now the anxiety attacks signaled the entrance of a terrible presence. This ghoul with a blaring, brutalizing masculine voice stalked me night and day. It sliced me with insults, then chewed me up and spit me out like a repulsive obscenity. The only way to keep him quiet was to binge and purge. The calming that settled through my body after bingeing and purging felt like being surrounded by a huge, protective, soundproof soap bubble. The divisiveness which tore me apart when I tried to resist the voice simply melted away during and following my binge/purge ritual. Actually, each time I binged and purged, I denied myself the opportunity to endure and integrate my feelings. I thus kept myself split off from my emotions, which were obviously struggling to be vented.

I was addicted and didn't even recognize it. I didn't even have a name for what was happening to me. (Bulimia research had barely begun.) I was ignorant to the insidiousness of the disease, and was confident that I could quit any time I decided I was ready. I was always ready "tomorrow."

Bulimia moved in and became my constant companion. How I functioned was a credit to my willpower. Outside I may have appeared competent, but inside I was falling apart. The more gluttonous I became, the more deceitful I became. The more deceitful I became, the more shamed I became. The more shamed I became, the more I needed to eat. It was an endless merry-go- round.

As the years went by and the addiction ruled my life, I engaged in some pretty risky behavior. Sometimes I would start bingeing at work about ten a.m. and then at noon, during lunch break, I would drive to a gas station, park my car toward the rear of the business, and sneak into the rest room for 20 or so minutes. When this became suspicious, I hovered around the rest room at work and when it was empty, I scurried inside and did my thing. Bingeing and purging at work became too strenuous, so I eventually quit eating lunch.

Willie was the last person I wanted to know about my addiction, so keeping it from him was most important. I lived in terror that Willie would leave me, so it was imperative that I always act in control. (Another sign of my insecurity.) In the twelve-and-a-half years we were married, he only caught me purging once and mandated, "Don't let me ever catch you doing this again!" Well, he never did.

Furthermore, no mention of my behavior was ever brought up between us again.

He had to have known what I was doing! Maybe that's why he was home less and less in the last six years of our marriage.

Every Sunday afternoon I spent bent over my plastic turquoise dish pan. We ate lunch with his family every Sunday, and Willie's mother was a fantastic, old-fashioned cook. I just couldn't stop feeding my face. When Willie and I returned to our house, he would stretch out on the sofa to watch football, and I would burrow in the back bedroom with the door locked. There I would stuff down some more of my hidden cache of food, and then vomit. It was sickening. I would position myself on my knees, bend over the turquoise pan, press my abdomen with my left hand, while sticking my right index finger down my throat. If Willie came to the door, I grabbed my hand towel, frantically wiped my mouth, right hand and wrist of dripping saliva and digesting food, and slid the turquoise pan along with the towel under the bed. My face was red due to the strain and the smell was putrid, but he never commented, much to my relief.

After the ballgame, he left to meet his friends and they rehashed the game. As soon as he shut the door to leave the house, I was tidying up. I poured my panful of vomit down the toilet, rinsed my towel, and sprayed deodorizer in the bedroom. All ready until next Sunday!

On those rare days when he would not meet with the guys, I brazenly dumped my refuse amid the tall weeds at the edge of our property. When that seemed too hazardous, I waddled the one block up to the First Methodist Church and took advantage of their bathroom facilities.

Parties required careful planning. Because I never wanted a bulging stomach for longer than three hours (the average duration of a binge) I maintained a wide berth between myself and the hors d'oeuvre table. About two hours before I anticipated our departure from the party, I cautiously closed in on the food. I was very discreet, taking only small amounts on my plate. The problem was I hovered for the rest of the evening within six feet of the table and refilled my plate time after time. Social gatherings lost their pleasure value and became just another torture chamber where I was battling for control.

When my bingeing and purging became a twice-a-day affair, I discovered it served the additional function of an appetite suppressant. A binge/purge at five a.m. quashed my hunger until four p.m. But eating nothing all day only increased the demand for nourishment once I acknowledged my hunger. As my hunger rumbled at the end of the day, so did the ghoul inside me. To silence them both, I binged and purged at night.

I also had to become more creative in hiding my habit. My excuses for the absence of food which was there one day and gone the next became ludicrous. "Would you believe that mice got into the cake and nibbled the frosting, so I threw it out," I expounded. "The cherry dessert? Oh, I gave half to the widow down the street." "You must be mistaken. There were only a few chips left in the bag and I had them with my sandwich for supper." It was crazy!

The compulsion became so strong that I found myself bingeing after Willie was in bed. I would think that I could innocently have one piece of chocolate cake. Not so. I would end up eating the entire sheet cake, a half-gallon of ice cream, countless slices of bread and butter, and several handfuls of potato chips.

What was I to do now? I could not possibly vomit in the bathroom. Willie might hear me. The bank! The bank was just across the street, and I could use their bathroom in total privacy, I schemed.

Furtively I reached into Willie's slacks pocket, eased out his keys ever so quietly, tiptoed out of the bedroom and out of the house. I had sunk to my lowest, I thought.

I only went to the bank about three times. It felt so fraudulent I couldn't live with my conscience.

The senselessness about my suffering was that I was under a psychiatrist's care, and I could have confided in him. My decision not to trust was indicative of my immense shame. I drove to Montgomery once every two weeks for a 50-minute session. The doctor's diagnosis was unipolar depression, for which he prescribed medication.

Not until late 1979, after I had been his patient for nine years, did I tell him about my bingeing and purging. He suspected a facet of anorexia nervosa but was flabbergasted when I exposed my bulimic practices.

Providing the catalyst for our future split was the death of Daddy in March, 1978, after a year-and-nine-months' battle with liver cancer. I was shattered — completely and unwaveringly shattered. Throughout his illness I begged God to let me die instead. Daddy was serving the world, I believed, and I was a useless tag-along. I was furious at God for letting my father die. In my magical thinking, Daddy was going to live forever. In fact, the first month after his death I convinced myself he was not dead. I was a walking zombie, and, I think, in shock. I rejected everyone by oozing coldness. I even refused to speak at times. I could not understand why this person I adored was yanked away. I turned my back on God, friends, and husband and sentenced myself to death by an emotional cancer of my own.

The relationship that I had entered for life was gasping its last breath by August 1980. I wanted to save it. I loved Willie enough to try to make some changes. The only thing I knew to do was to get marriage counseling. I scheduled an appointment with Willie's approval, but as time drew nearer for our session, I guess Willie had second thoughts. He informed me he couldn't go. He said he thought I was the one with the problems and therapy would be more plausible for me on an individual basis. For the umpteenth time in my life, I passively accepted someone else's verdict about my life. The personal pain I remember having at that moment was exacerbated by a larger pain. In my gut I knew my marriage was over and there was nothing I could do to save it.

6

Divorce

ON SEPTEMBER 2, 1980, Willie asked me for a divorce. Even though I knew it was coming, I was shocked. Mechanically, I nodded my head in agreement and then my mind went blank, like a downed computer screen.

The next day I pulled myself together and announced to Willie that I would pack my things and be out of the house as soon as possible. He told me to take whatever possessions I wanted. I rejected any thoughts of alimony, wanting to be self- sufficient, although Willie reluctantly acquiesced to pay me $100 per month for a few months to supplement my meager salary.

Saturday, September 13, I backed my blue MGB sports car out of the garage of our new house, feeling as if Jack the Ripper had sliced me from throat to navel. Nine months to this very day, Willie and I and our Cocker Spaniel had moved into our beautiful, long-awaited, new home. I wanted to cry and never stop. It was a black, black day.

Montgomery became my temporary abode until I quit work on November 26 and returned to Oklahoma.

My calendar for this period lists only cryptic clues as to my state of mind. "Rather depressed," I scribbled on a Monday. "More depressed" followed by "Very depressed" were etched on subsequent days.

My weight, which was 94 pounds when I left Willie, dropped to 90 pounds in Montgomery. My bingeing and purging escalated to a savageness. I absolutely did not want to deal with what had happened to me and Willie. Assuming total responsibility for the breakup, I condemned myself as an insufferable louse. I was afraid if I ever tapped into the pain, it would literally kill me. So, to keep my feelings at bay, I increased my calisthenics to one hour every morning and fell into a pattern of back-to-back binges and purges at night. Food became a contaminant to my already dirty body. I could binge and purge three times in a row and would have gone for a fourth if I hadn't been so exhausted.

My second addiction developed at this point, as well. Alcohol could numb me effectively, and since I didn't seem to have hangovers, I could guzzle a bottle of cheap wine in the evening and still remain highly functional at work the next day. Mostly, though, I restricted my drinking to weekends. Nevertheless, dependency on this crutch was established, and I would become a full-blown alcoholic by 1985.

Hopeful that things would be better once I settled in Oklahoma, my mood lifted somewhat as I wrapped things up in Alabama and drove back to my home state.

Indeed, life did have some thrilling packages awaiting me, but I still had lots and lots to learn!

7

Moving On

EDMOND, OKLAHOMA, WAS MY CHOICE as the launching pad of my new life. I scouted for and selected my own apartment in December and began my job January 7, 1981, as secretary to the ROTC Department at the local university. I was deliriously pleased with my courage and ingenuity of the past fifteen weeks. After all, I had never been on my own before, so every task became a challenge.

My job, though rather tedious and boring as far as work load, was immensely satisfying and comforting as far as personnel. I was the only female on the staff so I received all the attention. It was the healthy attention I had craved from men all my life. They respected me; they joked with me; they listened to me. I credit those guys with a major hunk of my healing during the next two and a half years. They were like family to me, and I will always hold them tenderly in my memory.

One of the officers, a young Captain named Douglas Merkel, took my breath away the very first time I saw him. My breathlessness was not a feeling of joy, however. It scared me silly. I was not about to get involved on the rebound with another man, and I definitely was never going to remarry. I had had it with men! Besides, I was a divorcee, which was still a stigma in 1980, and Doug was a Catholic.

What was I worried about? I planned to work from 7:30 a.m. until 4:30 p.m., attend classes at night, and study all weekend. Studying would not cease until I got my doctorate, and then I would practice psychotherapy. The outline I wrote for my life and the outline the Universe had in store for me were two different agendas.

By June, I felt stronger in some respects and weaker in others. At least I wasn't crying at the drop of a hat in the grocery store, the bank, at work, or in class. One year had to pass, though, before certain songs, blue jays squawking, changing seasons, birthdays, anniversaries, football games, hot dogs, and Cocker Spaniels didn't painfully remind me that I was half of what was once a whole. I was in therapy once a week, actually talking about my feelings and my bulimia. My drinking had subsided to social events on weekends. Thanks to two meals a day, my weight slowly increased by two-pound increments so that by the time I left Edmond in 1983, I weighed 100 pounds. Yet I remained in the clutches of bulimia as much as ever.

What I would buy to eat, where I would eat, and how much I could allow myself to eat were constantly on my mind. Grocery shopping became horrendous. I always had a list but once I was cruising down the aisles, everything beckoned to me. It was as if each can, each bottle, each box, each cellophane package became a miniature octopus, arms curling and swaying and enticing me to buy them. My agreement with myself was that I would buy groceries only once a week, and then only buy healthy foods. I reasoned that if there were skim milk, cottage cheese, tuna fish, fresh vegetables, and fruit in the apartment, I wouldn't be tempted to binge/purge. Again I was oblivious to the fact that my eating disorder had nothing to do with what kind of food was around. So, admirable as it sounds, this plan collapsed the first week I implemented it.

One day, after stocking my shelves with wholesome edibles, the undeniable urge for sweets struck. I whirled into the grocery store, and like a tornado, scooped up enough cookies, pastries, and candy to feed seventy Halloween trick-or-treaters.

To counter this impulse buying, I started carrying only my checkbook in my purse, leaving my bills and change in my apartment. Alas, this strategy backfired, too, as I would feel so desperate for my food fix, I would write a check for my goodies.

I was truly concerned about my uncontrollable addiction to food, as my journal reflects:

> *I am so tired tonight! This was to be the end of my bulimia, but somehow the fear of the emptiness settled upon me. I am so low now — my life seems to have no purpose. I really feel blue and worthless. Why or what am I running from? Why do I feel so inferior and so strangely frightened and insecure? I feel so much hate for myself. What is my problem? Why do I feel like screaming at everyone — telling them to leave me alone. I HATE this bulimia but WHY can't I stop it? Why do I hate myself SO much? I am so tired of hating life — why is it so hard for me? Why can't I learn to laugh? Why am I so serious? Am I too lazy to work at being happy or do I enjoy this misery? WHY can't I take things as they come? Other people have problems but they've learned how to evaluate them — how to cope. I never learned how to face crises. I soon turned to food for solace and companionship and now it is an addiction. Now I must face problems like an adult. I must FACE pain, tears, sorrow, disappointment.*

By 1982, I knew full well the ramifications of bulimia, but health hazards, even the prospect of death, didn't curtail my bingeing and purging. If anything, their awareness made me more frantic.

My teeth seemed to be my primary concern because I felt I had beautiful, strong teeth, and I could see evidence of slight erosion on the outside of my bottom molars. To protect my teeth from further deterioration, laxatives seemed to be the logical answer.

I furtively slid the package of Ex-Lax across the drug store counter one Friday afternoon and ingested two squares the following Saturday morning. They did practically nothing for me (thank goodness!), so I threw away the remaining supply that night and never used another laxative.

Intensifying my already elevated fear level about being alone was a recurrent nightmare which propelled me out of sleep and into wakefulness where I was yelling and thrashing about on my bed. A huge tarantula would bite my right jugular vein in my neck and cling there chewing and sucking out my blood. I had never been afraid of spiders before this dream, but after two episodes I became terrified of them. The value of dream interpretation was unknown to me at this time, so I ignored the message. If I had probed into the dream's symbolism, I could have gained some valuable information and perhaps not been terrorized by this same dream for the next eight years.

My expanding involvement with Doug left me flip-flopping between rapture and despondency. He was generous, kind, adventuresome, and we had lots of fun together. He was also aloof and quiet and somewhat secretive. It wasn't long before I felt a real void when he wasn't with me. I began repeating the same pleasing behavior in an attempt to keep him hanging around in my life. Unconsciously, I was acting on the antiquated tape, "A woman is nothing without a husband." I thought if I could just be perfect and doting enough, he would love me. When he resisted my pushes for commitment, I felt angry and frustrated. "Why was I bothering with someone who wouldn't be open and honest with me?" I asked. I didn't comprehend that Doug was a mirror for my own inability to trust. The problem was not Doug's but mine.

My pattern, still hidden to my awareness, was to chase (out of a frenzied fear of loneliness) and then withdraw (out of an equally frenzied fear of intimacy).

Though our courtship might have been marred by this mutual fear of being real with each other, we developed strong bonds.

It was a melancholy day, indeed, when Doug departed for his next assignment in Fayetteville, North Carolina, on December 20, 1982. I honestly thought I had been taken for the biggest ride of my life, and that this guy was a love-'em-and-leave-'em type whom I would never see again despite his promise of a future rendezvous.

Was I ever wrong! Doug has proven to be a loyal man in my life.

Off To Africa

DECEMBER 30, 1982, 8:55 p.m., my diary sings:

> *Doug called and said, "I love you!" He said it! He said it!*

Later entry, 11:35 p.m., I added:

> *Doug called back and asked me to marry him! I said yes!!*

My life was popping now, and my adrenalin would keep me on a wild high for the next month. I shut out that nagging sensation that something wasn't quite right — that I wasn't ready for this step quite yet — that I was on a tidal wave and no longer in control.

I had some unfinished business with Doug that now had to be revealed. I had to tell him about my bulimia. I had deliberately kept this secret from him because I felt there was no need to tell him until I knew he was serious about me. Until now he had hedged speaking of love and had only given me obscure hints.

Late one evening in the hushed silence of my apartment, on the desk I had had since seventh grade, I wrote Doug a letter explaining my addiction to food and enclosing a copy of Cherry O'Neill's *Starving For Attention*. Her book had been such a comfort to me, and I wanted Doug to see how an eating disorder could ravage an individual as well as a family. This letter was excruciating for me to write because I felt that now that I had exposed my "badness," Doug would see me as evil and dump me. Why would any man hang this albatross around his neck when the sea was filled with fresh, vigorous, young fish? I wiped my tears on my sleeve and with resignation thought, This will finish us up for sure.

To my surprise, Doug responded with compassion and, as always, made me chuckle with his comment, "I wondered why you were so thin." He said not to worry, adding, "There is nothing you could do that would make me stop loving you." He assured me we would lick this thing together.

I was dumfounded! Where were the accusations, the judgments, the cold shoulder?

The wedding was set for March 26, 1983, so that preparations could be completed before our July departure to Tunisia, Africa, Doug's next assignment.

One last unpleasantry awaited my attention in Edmond. At the foot of my bed was a footlocker containing mementos of my first marriage, poems and essays and short stories I had written, and personal items belonging to Daddy that Mother had given me. It was time. I knew I was ready.

For three or four hours on a Saturday, I sifted through my first love affair, the day we chose our wedding bands, the wedding book, the pictures of those important and those everyday happenings, drawings and compositions expressing my pain and confusion, sympathy cards from Daddy's death, and even clothing I had squirreled away. Part of me wanted to fling it all back inside the trunk, shut the lid, lock it, and scoot it into some dark, forgotten corner. The other part of me knew I had to let go and replace death with life — endings with beginnings — dark with light.

I filled several grocery sacks to the rim and carted them out to the public dumpster. They crashed atop other discarded refuse, tumbled on their sides, and spilled some of my treasures. I felt sick. I felt like I wanted to cry and cry and cry and never stop . . . but I didn't. I should have, because that unacknowledged grief and rage would continue seething.

The whirlwind of activities until Doug and I arrived in Tunis prevented me from moping too long. I was so excited about going to Africa, but scared at the same time. At heart I am an adventuress, and I love traveling and learning about other cultures. What I wasn't prepared for was living in a strange country. Touring versus residing in a foreign land are two opposite experiences.

Plus, I was being very shortsighted to think that a geographical change could cure my bulimia and that I would suddenly use all this free time to draw, paint, write and study French.

True, while in Edmond, I had acquired some skills and interests that enhanced my ego, but my knowledge of my Inner Self remained as barren as a sand dune. I was kidding myself big-time in thinking that this journey would be my ticket to freedom!

9

Tunis, Tunisia

OUR PRE-ARRIVAL SCHEDULE to Africa was feverish. I joined Doug in Fayetteville, North Carolina, after terminating my job in Edmond. He graduated from his training course, we visited each of our families one last time, took our honeymoon in the Bahamas, completed military briefings and moving arrangements in Washington, D.C., and New Jersey, and toured Paris, France, before landing at the Tunis airport in late July of 1983.

Naturally, with all this travel, my control over what I ate was rare. We were being wined and dined, and food and alcohol abated our apprehensions about this overseas duty. It was easier not to dwell on our fears, so we shoveled escapist activities over them.

I was more distraught with anxiety than I realized, so to maintain my thinness, and thus some order in my life, my bingeing and purging worsened. My panic attacks increased to at least three a day and always preceded a meal. Yet I veiled my insecurities and plowed headstrong with smiles and cordiality. Inside, I was second-guessing my choice to remarry. What had I gotten myself into?

My journal entry for the day after our arrival coldly lists my reactions:

Depressed, angry, tired, frightened, resentful.

The duality struggle within me broke the surface. I harbored negativity from the first second while simultaneously wanting to find the positive aspects of this once-in-a-lifetime adventure. Sadly, I simply did not have the inner strengths nor the external tools required to carry me through what was to become an acute crisis period in my life.

By September, Doug and I both were feeling very stressed. As newlyweds we were trying to get to know each other plus a completely different culture. On top of this was a job change for Doug and a lifestyle change for me.

Up until now, I had always worked or been in school. I felt restless and useless. To fill my endless hours, I enrolled in correspondence classes and volunteered at the tiny, musty American library across from the American Embassy.

Also, I binged and purged! I was totally a victim by now, not only of my bulimia but of alcoholism. I binged at breakfast, lunch, and supper. I vomited two to three hours later after each meal. Southern Comfort and ginger ale were mixed at 4:00 p.m. each afternoon and refills continued until 8:00 p.m. I was self- destructing but too ashamed to admit that I couldn't handle what the other military wives seemed to be taking one hour at a time. Patience was not my virtue.

I turned to the person whose nurturing felt so needed. I wrote my mother a tearful, anguishing letter in which my anger flowed like blood from a fresh cut. I was homesick and wanted to be cuddled like a lonely child. Since she had always bolstered my spirits while I was in Edmond, I automatically presumed she would hold my hand during this debacle. Her response sent me spiraling into a frenzy of despair. I wrote:

> *Day before yesterday I received a scathing reply to a letter I wrote Mother in which she condemned me for being so immature and lectured me on how "grateful" I should be to have a man! Furthermore, my "compulsion with food" could be eliminated with a little more self-control! (She has never ad-*

*mitted I had anorexia nor that I have bulimia.)
My first reaction was hurt, pain — deep, cutting
hurt. I cried for two hours. Then I felt im-
measurable rage. A rage so scary I could have
slapped her and screamed in her face. How the hell
can she lecture me when she can't even begin to
understand what I am experiencing over here!! I
hate her! I hate her!*

My notations continue:

Something clicked! I have been reading My
Mother/Myself *, and the authoress said when she
was little she never let herself express the words "I
hate you" to her mother for fear of losing that love;
therefore, the authoress redirected the statement
toward herself to punish herself for such an un-
grateful thought. BINGO!!! What had I been doing
all my life? Just that!! Desperately craving love,
wanting to please and be perfect, terrified of doing
something so displeasurable my parents wouldn't
love me anymore! I do things sometimes and
make myself a victim. I must fight depression. I
give up too often. I get tired. But if I can make some
headway while in Tunis, if I can be introspective
enough, I can really grow here. I realize now
everyone gets lonely. I've talked to both sexes, and
they have all gone through hell here. I thought
more successful people were not as susceptible, but
I was wrong. Oddly enough, last night I was reading an article about Albert Einstein. He said,
"Though I have world acclaim, I get so lonely."
That hit me like a ton of bricks. I have always run
away from feeling. I have decided I will feel everything now.*

In moving to Tunisia, I had stripped myself of all familiar
cultural, familial, and therapeutic supports with the excep-
tion of my husband. Consequently, I was emotionally vulnerable, which meant that I was terribly afraid. Awakened
were my Inner Child's fear of loss of love and her fear of

not surviving. I masqueraded my fear with anger. Independence dangled at my finger tips, but my feet were still crippled by dependency, so moving forward while in Tunis was a clumsy lunge. I fell flat on my face.

My efforts were brave, but the ball and chain of bulimia rapidly sapped my resolve. My journal testifies to my internal war:

I'm sitting here eating candy-coated almonds. WHY? Why — what — am I feeling that I must stuff? Anger — yes. I'm angry at me for being such a coward. Read an article about B. F. Skinner yesterday. He said even he didn't like himself. Funny. Another famous person dissatisfied. Life is hard for everyone. I feel like I could cry forever today.

Doug senses the fear I have of being loved and my fear to express love. Yet he still remains. Could his love be this faithful? I am suspicious and afraid to depend on anyone. Hence, I act stubborn and defensive.

Doug said yesterday Collette asked him why we bought so much food. I felt so ashamed inside that he should have to fabricate lies to cover my habit. It is okay for me to lie — it's my problem. I felt a surge of hate pulse through my body. Why do you do this? Other people are beginning to notice. You're no good! I pounded these thoughts to myself. Out loud and in a hostile voice I addressed Doug, "Did you tell her it was your wife? She's a pig!" I wanted to run and hide and cry and cry. Instead, I shut the bathroom door and vomited my supper — the supper I vowed not to eat at 4:30 p.m. I don't want to vomit ever again! I want to quit! Then I laughed at myself. How many zillion times had I cried to do that!!!

We had our first fresh, REAL beef tonight. We bought two huge standing rib steaks from the "blue butcher." They were a little tough, but they were real beef. What a treat! I even laughed out loud and jumped in the air when I saw them on Doug's homemade grill. I wanted desperately to relax and enjoy my meat, but I didn't. Before the first bite, I was chastising myself with, "You don't need to eat supper. You're 102 pounds — overweight!! You will have to vomit." I did. Felt very tired and defeated. Occasionally in Edmond, I would let myself enjoy one steak supper a week. Over here — the punishment when I eat is every meal!! I'm tired of vomiting.

Several days later I grappled with myself:

Have been very low since Sunday. Want to cry constantly. I also need help with this awful bulimia! I am so tired yet my self-punishment becomes more ruthless each day. The hours are interminable with nothing to do. It is up to me to fill them, right? Right!! I can't budge. All I want to do is eat, hide, and cry. This is no good! I feel like screaming! I want to punish myself into oblivion. In fact, I hope bulimia does kill me. I feel very hopeless. I can't convey my distress on this paper. I want to cry and cry and cry!!

Got a little drunk last night on top of my gorging. Liquor makes the homesickness and the anger less potent.

Here I sit gorged, hating myself, and wanting to cry, cry, cry. My life is wasting away, and I can't take charge of it! What has happened to my veracity, my persistence, my thoroughness? I have become lazy and waste time. I'll never get over this bulimia. All I think about is food! I feel so afraid and alone and helpless.

Finally, Doug and I had a serious, honest talk, and each of us admitted that we were miserable in Tunisia. The assignment was not appropriate for Doug, and he was ready to return to the States. At long last, I reconciled to the fact that I alone could not rout out my eating disorder. I needed to commit myself to healing once and for all.

There would not be a gentle way to transfer out, either. I had to fly to Germany and obtain an official document from an Army psychiatrist stating that my illness was such that only stateside treatment would suffice.

My humiliation reached its pinnacle as I walked out of that West German hospital that crisp fall afternoon. Nothing would be mentioned in the records about Doug's dissatisfaction with the tour of duty. I would be the scapegoat. I felt angry and ashamed and imagined a placard on my chest emblazoned with the giant message, "REJECT. CERTIFIABLY BULIMIC."

10

Columbus, Georgia

LEARNING THAT WE WOULD BE SENT to Ft. Benning, Georgia, filled me with dread. When I left Alabama in 1980, I was sure I would never return to that vicinity. Columbus, the home city of Ft. Benning, was right across the river from Alabama!

Well, first things first. I was so happy to be back in the United States, I decided to deal with my "old life" when the time came. There were too many things to do to prepare for the present life.

Since Doug was compelled to report to duty immediately, apartment hunting became my responsibility. By intuition alone, I plucked what, to me, proved to be the "richest" complex in Columbus. It was a small group of apartments in the Wynnton area of the city. The bonds I wove with many of the residents remain some of the most precious in my life. Those people were so friendly and loving I felt like I had been accepted into a special family.

My two primary goals during this three-year stint were to obtain my B.S. degree in psychology and to conquer my fourteen- year struggle with bulimia. I enrolled in classes at Columbus College, and I "found" a therapist. Let me explain.

CHAMPUS, the military insurance we used, was approved at a private psychiatric clinic in our neighborhood, so I presented my records to the director and he arbitrarily assigned me to a staff psychologist named Dr. Steve Felker. For the first time since I had been divorced, I now had insurance. Scarcity, especially with money, was one of my major emotional roadblocks, and having insurance freed me considerably of guilt feelings. Brazenly, I advocated for two sessions a week and maintained this schedule until July, 1984, when only one session was needed.

Dr. Felker appealed to me the instant I saw him. He was young, handsome, and commanding in his quietness. He reminded me of a cross between Omar Sharif and John Stossel, a reporter for "20/20." After only one month, I trusted Dr. Felker as I had trusted no man in my life. I unloaded everything on him, over and over, time after time, and he always met me each week with unconditional understanding. This trust factor initiated much of the healing I required on my issues with men. He championed my efforts, but he didn't coddle me. Because of his nudging, I expanded my therapeutic support system by joining a therapy group, an eating disorders support group, and Overeaters Anonymous. Dr. Felker was another of the many benevolent gifts given to me in Columbus.

Academic life, as usual, became a safari through the sludge. I entered courses with my most ambitious zeal to date, registering for winter, spring, summer, and fall quarters until I graduated. I studied hard and learned a lot. My professors were demanding yet likable, and for the first time in my life, I chatted informally with some of them and began to see them as having feelings and problems like everyone else. Oh, sure, I bitched about unfair questions on tests, lengthy papers, and time-consuming projects. By making them responsible for any of my grades below 95, I could preserve my illusion of my perfection.

Until now, just imagining perfection could rekindle my motivation every time it lagged, but fissures had started creeping into my hard-nosed philosophy. As I learned more through my studies, I observed how imperfect all humans were. Disheartening as this realization was, it prompted me to sporadically re-examine, and to consider lowering, my own expectations. I pondered, "Am I so exacting that I will accept someone only as long as they conform to my perfect standards? That is asking for a lifetime of disappointment."

Soon a B.S. in psychology was not a lofty enough goal. I wanted a Ph.D. in counseling psychology so that I could "really help" sufferers of eating disorders. Perhaps I could even work for ANAD, National Association of Anorexia Nervosa and Associated Disorders, since I admired Vivian Meehan, the president, so much. An admirable pursuit on the surface.

The pressure I placed on myself to make straight "A's" became more ferocious than ever. I didn't laugh or celebrate small accomplishments. I pulled out my mental whipping boy, The Punisher, and he bludgeoned me with thoughts that nothing was ever perfect enough and that time spent congratulating myself over a success was wasted time. Pushing myself until I had achieved all my dreams was the true magnanimous path, and only then would I be allowed to relax.

Needless to say, I graduated from Columbus College *summa cum laude* with a 3.94 grade point average and my Phi Kappa Phi honor society ribbon pinned to my gown. I felt like I held the world in my hands, but my body was being strangled by my addictions.

Naturally, with the lid sealed on my pressure-cooker life, the steam had to escape somehow. My old standbys, bulimia and alcohol, were right there.

Doug was eating and drinking with me, but I still felt tremendous guilt. I would have two gin and tonics and would munch chips and dip for an hour before he came home from work. We sat down to supper with seconds and, for me, thirds and fourths, and then I would retreat to my books where, while studying, I would finish off with cookies or candy bars I had stashed in my desk drawers. Doug was left alone with his drinks downstairs to watch television or to read. All of this was justified in my mind in the name of graduating from college with a superior standing. But what havoc was I wreaking in the longterm for my body and my marriage?

My daily alcohol abuse was curtailed drastically in late 1984, all because it hit me that the one organ I valued above all the rest was the very one I was destroying: my brain.

I presented myself to my Tests and Measurements class one cold November day, but due to a fuzzy, throbbing head from too much gin the night before, I chose to sit on the farthest and highest tier of the auditorium-type classroom. Normally, I sat on the second row from the podium, not wanting to miss a word. This day I didn't care if the professor died, or if I died, for that matter. I was really down on life in general.

The lecture commenced. Every word bounced off my forehead and temples, setting up wave after wave of pain inside my skull. "Why is he shouting so loudly?" I chuckled to myself. Gradually, I realized the professor was speaking at his normal volume. "You've got a hangover, Suzy, and it's ugly! There is nothing funny about this! How many brain cells do you think you exterminate with every drinking binge? Your brain is your future. Your brain is your life!" I heard myself thinking.

By the time I got home that afternoon, I had decided my brain was too valuable to be treated like a pickle jar. No more hard liquor for me — only wine, and then only on Friday and Saturday nights.

By 1987, two or three glasses of wine a week were all I ever drank, if I even chose to have that much. Until then it took one more very disappointing and excruciating experience to make me sober up completely.

In September, 1986, I enrolled in the Masters of Social Work program at the University of Georgia. It was a huge commitment which Doug and I had discussed at great length. I wanted this degree badly and was terribly impressed with the faculty and the curriculum at the University of Georgia. I moved to Athens where I lived during the week. I drove the three and a half hours back to Columbus every weekend.

Everyone supported me except myself. The Pusher and The Punisher parts of my personality emerged with a vengeance. Once more grades outweighed knowledge, and I was squeezing myself with pressure.

Before long, I was including a bottle of wine in my evening binge/purge. I knew exactly what I was doing but told myself that after a few weeks when I felt more comfortable with my classmates and the schedule, I would drop the bingeing and purging as well as the drinking. Who was I kidding? This pattern was identical to my undergraduate pattern.

My grades were solid "A's" and "B's," and I wanted desperately to continue, but I had made a vow to myself when I enrolled. "I will not push for straight 'A's,' and if I start bingeing and purging and drinking every night, I will quit the program. I will not use these crutches to get me through graduate school," I said.

Even with the help of a weekly university counseling session, I continued my evening activities. By the middle of October, I saw that my habits were not changing, so I withdrew, thinking, "You will rout out this bulimia before you ever return to another classroom!"

I slipped on this promise, but I have not abused alcohol since that time.

11

My First Breakthrough

LAMENTABLY, THE FOOD ADDICTION did not fall away
as conveniently as the alcohol addiction. I was angry and
despondent about this, too, and confided to Dr. Felker that
I didn't think I was ever going to get rid of the bulimia. He
merely gazed at me and said in his tender way, "Maybe you
shouldn't be viewing success in terms of the decline and
eventual termination of the number of times you binge and
purge. You are making considerable advancement in social
interactions, in emotional awareness, and in psychological
strengths. Your bulimia may very well be the last symptom
to dissolve."

This advice comforted me greatly and helped me to be
more patient with myself.

When I look back on the years 1984-1986, I realize they
were a time for me to lay the first groundwork for my
healing. I was reading everything I could find on eating
disorders. I was in therapy. I was co-leader in the eating
disorders group and a frequent leader for one Overeaters
Anonymous group. When I wasn't involved directly with
some support mechanism, I was questioning on my own.
But I felt like I was missing some very key elements. I was
fumbling in the dark. Until, that is, I read *The Deadly Diet,
Recovering From Anorexia & Bulimia* by Dr. Terence J.
Sandbek. This book cleared away the gray and gave me

some tangible tools to implement in my battle with my bulimia.

I am so glad I ordered a copy of his book even though I did so with a cynical attitude. "Might as well investigate what this one has to offer," I yawned.

For the first time, someone identified the creature that screamed in my head. Dr. Sandbek simply calls this one's Voice.

Secondly, he lists six primary feelings and their corresponding thought patterns. It was as if he had been living in my head and written down my exact thoughts. Now I could pinpoint a feeling by the thought which was running through my head. Can you imagine what a relief it was to be able to identify which feeling I was feeling?

I continued to suffer from panic attacks, but, at least, I had something concrete to use in order to slow the spinning. I was not carried away so overwhelmingly in that whirlpool of confusion and disorientation.

Thirdly, Dr. Sandbek provides affirmations and self-help exercises so the reader can become proficient at coping with feelings aroused before, during, or after various uncomfortable situations.

The Deadly Diet was a candle in the darkness for me and became my "Bible." I still refresh myself with its contents periodically.

Thank you, Dr. Sandbek!

12

Columbus, Good-Bye

IN NOVEMBER, 1986, Doug had the opportunity to accept an assignment opening in January, 1987, in Midwest City, Oklahoma. We really didn't think twice about not returning to Oklahoma as we had enjoyed our time there together before. We could buy a house, explore things we missed first time around, and I could be closer to my mother, my sisters, and their families. Visions of cozy family gatherings filled my fantasies while I tended to the drudgery of packing.

Leaving my friends, my groups, and Dr. Felker was a million times harder than I had thought.

My Overeaters Anonymous groups gave me hugs and warm wishes. It was through this organization that I made my first wobbling steps into spirituality. Soured on organized religion and skeptical of God as a judgmental, masculine, human form, I found peace with the idea of a Higher Power. At this time, my Higher Power was the ocean and the beach.

My eating disorders support group bought a card, and each person signed it. That card remains on my desk, sending me love every time I look at it.

But parting with my resource person and co-leader, Rose Allinder, was the saddest. Rose had been there from the beginning with encouragement and her own example as a strong, female role model. She was and is ahead of her time. She forced me to scrutinize the issue of alcohol in my family. She introduced me to the wounded Inner Child concept. And she was keen on women regaining their personal power.

Severing ties with Dr. Felker was the most painful. He had become a true bulwark in my life. Much to my surprise, he told me that I had given him something, too. He commented in our last session, "You reaffirmed my faith in the fighting spirit. You never gave up. You kept fighting."

As we exchanged a final hug, he told me I was ready to fly. He was absolutely correct!

13

Reality Hits

IF I WAS READY TO FLY, it certainly didn't feel like it. What I imagined as delightful became one huge horror story once I was in Oklahoma. "This is not the way I pictured things to be! What has happened to me?" I kept screaming to myself. I was lonely, listless, depressed, and so resentful I could have spit on people just as easily as look at them.

I was bitter at everything and harped on comparisons between Edmond/Oklahoma City and Columbus. The comfortable home we bought north of Edmond was far away from town and necessitated a thirty-minute drive on a congested freeway to Oklahoma City. In Columbus, the grocery store, my support groups, Dr. Felker's office, the college, the cleaners, the gas station, the fitness club, the post office, and the shopping centers were only ten minutes away on residential streets.

Temperatures were freezing and there was snow on the ground when we moved into our house in February. Winter days were usually mild in Columbus.

Furthermore, a house required more maintenance than an apartment, and suddenly I was drained at the thought of all the housework and yard work.

Doug had a job to occupy his time for the next four years. What was I supposed to do? Doug was working 10-12 hours a day plus most weekends so we had no leisure time together for fun outings like we did in Columbus.

Most importantly, I had no friends, no support system in Oklahoma. The dearest friends I had ever made since I left home at age 18 were now 1,000 miles away. Making friends was no small feat for me. I am guarded and hesitant about risking involvement.

I was disconsolate. I realized I was the recipient of my own need to control. The idealized picture I created about returning to Oklahoma was my usual, crafty self-deception.

I loaded myself with "shoulds." I should have let Doug reconsider this assignment instead of pushing to accept it. I should have known one cannot recapture the past. I should have appreciated what and who I had in Columbus. I should not have been so blind.

What was done was done. It was up to me to be productive or to remain belligerent. Though I arranged a schedule for myself, I was only putting one foot in front of the other. It was like treading in molasses.

Volunteer work at a local bookstore, reading for the Library of the Blind, and assisting at a social service facility held some of my boredom at bay. I could not click with anyone, and my separateness bothered me greatly. I wanted friends, but fear of committing for only four years caused me to recoil in pain. I am sure my body language shouted, "Stay away!"

I needed to feel more than just useful. I wanted to be "doing something important." With my perspective at this time, that meant only one direction: school. The University of Oklahoma had an MSW program, so I filed my paperwork and was accepted for the fall term beginning in August. My guilt vanished and I felt much more secure knowing that I now had a place where I belonged.

The situation on the food front had deteriorated again with the disruption of the move. Within a month of moving into the house, I had reinstituted two, and sometimes three, regimented meals a day, carefully recording every calorie and making sure I didn't exceed 1200 calories. I was feeling "safe" only at 100 pounds and maintained this weight by frequently eliminating supper.

A change, though not to my liking, was peeping through. A binge/purge was no longer suppressing my appetite. I remained as ravenous after a binge/purge as before. I seemed to crave more and more and more. I wanted all the meat in the grocery store, all the candy at the sweet shop, and all the ice cream at the dairy bar. I groan when I review my binge list for February 28, 1987:

1 - 3-pound roast with fat
1 - large frozen combo pizza
1 - angel food cake
1 - 12-ounce tub frozen dairy topping
1 - 12-ounce package Brach's chocolate stars
1 - 12-ounce package coconut patties
1 - box peanut and caramel popcorn
12 - caramel sweet rolls

How empty I was! I knew it, too. The war inside me was like World War III. On one hand, I was trying to be responsible by eating three meals a day, repeating my affirmations, attending OA, Al-Anon, and ACOA meetings, and writing in my journal about what and why I was feeling. On the other hand, my Voice was determined to keep me enslaved in negativity and helplessness. I felt like I was regressing instead of progressing.

In May, after concluding a 12-week outpatient program for my bulimia, I was no better than when I entered. I had worked so diligently and done and eaten everything I was told! If anything, I was now more vigilant than ever about what and how much I ate. My sense of "failure" increased my self-judgment. "What is wrong with me?" I would sob. "Why can't I get rid of this bulimia?"

I had come farther than I knew. My shell was cracking and my Inner Child was beginning to cry out with incredible rage, hurt, and neediness.

14

A Lifeline Appears

M AY 18, 1987:

Had first appointment with Dr. Kowalski.
Quite an intellectual but not condescending. His
excitement about life and ideas is contagious. He
senses a naturalness trying to come out of me. He
says perhaps I have a whole glob of emotions
ready to erupt, not just anger. I told him I feel so
empty inside — like I have no essence.

Dr. Kowalski saved my life. If he had not held me in his
loving, highly trained hands while I cracked wide open, I
might not be on track today. He reassured me I was not
going crazy, only passing through a pivotal life transition.
"Dr. K," as I nicknamed him, is a psychiatrist in Oklahoma
City. With him, I found someone who listened and truly
understood my struggle on the deepest levels. What's
more, he pegged many of my issues on the very first, brief
session. This guy knew what he was doing and he was
vivacious as well!

We talked initially about my bulimia, my pervasive fears,
my resentment of authority figures, and my panic attacks.
He said my panic attacks were probably a throwback to an
earlier time as a child when I felt intense feelings, such as
anger, sorrow, and fear. The feelings became all jumbled as
I grew up, and now when something triggered their tumult,

I experienced a panic attack. He suggested pantomime to help work through the feelings. This consisted of hurling my fists in the air, stomping my feet, squinching my eyes, and opening my mouth to emit silent screams. It didn't take long for vocalization to erupt, and I was soon crying and screaming. Next came the need to hit something, so Dr. K told me to pound on a pillow. I did and the release was instantaneous. Little Suzy was not merely angry. She was enraged!

She was also terrorized with the fear of being abandoned. When trying to go through my first panic attack, I had this experience:

> *I felt myself being swallowed by blackness. There was a sense of falling helplessly in a never-ending black canyon. I felt like there were NEVER going to be any loving, supportive arms to catch me EVER again. Then I was aware of a cavernous emptiness inside. I felt I was going to crumble, but I heard Little Suzy say, "I won't crumble. I will just have to take care of myself." Then I felt a cold hardening of my body. Was this the armor I wore to this day? Quickly, I returned to feelings. I entered the pain and fear inside the empty cavern. I discarded identification with Little Suzy and imagined Mother and Daddy. I empathized with their grief — their loss — their utter despair at Joe Ben's death. I cried deep, powerful sobs. I partially forgave them for not validating me. I understood THEIR void.*

Though grief suspended my passing through to the other side of this panic attack, I was very determined that one day I would, and, in so doing, I would free myself of this spinning terror.

By monitoring my reactions in the past to doctors, bosses, teachers, and businessmen, I realized that my resentment toward them stemmed from my anger with Daddy, who could be intolerant, stern, and controlling. I began noticing that same rebellion crop up more and more in my relationship with Doug, especially when he departed for work or for a business trip. Was I making Doug into an authority figure, too? Why did I immediately feel like bingeing and purging the mintue he left the house?

I thought about the nights as a young teenager when Mother and Daddy would go out to a party and leave me and my younger sister at home by ourselves for about three hours. I felt wild with excitement and heady at the thought of three hours of freedom. I did the things I felt I could not do while my parents were at home. I let the dog inside the house. I watched the scary late movie. I played records at full volume and danced. I giggled. I jumped on my bed. No censorship was exhilarating.

This dualistic nature of celebration and rebellion overcame me every time Doug said good-bye. I examined my head talk after several of his departures and was amazed. The Voice usually clattered like this, "Oh, boy! He's gone! Now you can have fun, fun, fun, and do whatever you want! Let go and relax! No one will be around to judge you! You can eat anything!"

On the adult level, I knew Doug would return from his absence, but what was happening on the Inner Child level? Maybe Little Suzy was experiencing the opposite of excitement. Maybe she was scared because his leaving felt like abandonment.

Bingo! The bells went off. I was dumbfounded when I hit that strident chord of abandonment.

Thereafter, every time Doug left the house for anything, I mentally put my arms around a vision of Little Suzy and repeated over and over, "You are safe. I am here. You will never be alone again." If need be, I read her a story or let her color or write. I indulged her need for my undivided attention.

After a year of practicing this behavior, I no longer binge and purge when Doug leaves home.

Since I wanted a concave shape between protruding hip bones, many of my binges and purges were precipitated by a belief that my abdomen was bulging. I named this belief "feeling fat." Dr. K had clear insight into this twisted thought. I never could have deduced such a theory on my own, but even as he explained it, I felt circuits in my brain clicking.

It was on one visit to Dr. K's office in June, 1987, and I was really battling with "feeling fat." He listened with care and then asked pointedly, "In each person's life, when is the time when he or she is soft and flabby and chubby?"

"When they are infants," I replied, wondering where in the world he was going with that question.

"Exactly," he smiled benevolently. "Babies are soft and flabby and fat, but they are not aware of their fatness. They are aware of their powerlessness. Crying to get attention can be ignored by caregivers. The only thing babies have control of is spitting out food!"

I sat there as if I had been electrocuted. My mind was quivering. He explained that when I am "feeling fat" my unconscious is remembering my state as a baby. I am remembering my powerlessness and fear. The fear is so intense I want to run away and binge/purge. A binge/purge is my adult metaphor for the child's temper tantrum. A child has a temper tantrum for four reasons: (1) hunger, (2) fatigue, (3) illness, and (4) fear of separateness. The disorganization of the child can be shown as rage in the adult.

For months, I chewed this cud of information that my bulimia was rooted in this childhood issue of powerlessness and its subsequent feelings of fear and confusion. I had been trying to ignore or eliminate Little Suzy's cries of expression, thus smothering my naturalness and becoming angrier and angrier.

Dr. K had one final seismological topic for me to explore: sexual abuse. Confident of his diagnosis of Post-traumatic Stress Disorder induced after Joe Ben's death, Dr. K, nevertheless, asked me to consider the possibility that my symptoms of depression, bulimia, survivor guilt, and fears of men and sex might also be fallout from sexual abuse. He reassured me that molestation might not be a factor in my own life, but he had seen many daughters who, when enmeshed with their mothers like I was, exhibited all the trauma for their mothers who had been raped and then repressed the event.

At first I was appalled. I couldn't even say the word "rape" much less think about the act. But I realized that as long as I was plying uncharted waters, I might as well explore every inlet. Dr. K and I were like any other doctor and patient trying to pinpoint the roots of a phantom illness. The worst scenario, as well as the most innocuous one, has to be given thoughtful attention. Each malady eliminated makes one less concern for the patient.

15

And The Walls
Come Tumbling Down

T O RECONSTRUCT SOMETHING, often it must first be
razed. Such was the case for my cognitive/behavioral structure. It had to smash to the floor of reality and break into
14,623 pieces, one piece for each day of my life. My fortieth
birthday marked the beginning of my plunge. Like a vase
teetering on the edge of a table top, I toppled into the
nothingness of myself, gaining speed as stresses felt more
and more overwhelming, and I felt helpless to prevent my
flying apart. I described it this way in my journal:

> On my 40th birthday I jumped off the cliff and
> started falling. I knew I had to just BE. I had to
> discard what felt safe and solid. Those things were
> not working for me. They worked for the Suzy
> ensnared in everyone else's expectations, values,
> and beliefs, not for the Suzy now breaking free. It
> feels as if I am an infant again restarting life.

As I neared impact, I became acutely aware of my
charred insides. With a sensitive art therapist, I had been
trying to draw and mold what I could not articulate with
words. My work was so primitive that I was glaringly aware
of a huge half of my brain that had been dormant.

I wrote honestly:

> *I feel dead inside. What have I done to myself?*
> *Where is my creative, happy self? Where have I lost*
> *myself along the way? My Voice gets crueler every*
> *minute. I want to break free and do fun things,*
> *but I choose to suffer rather than employ the adult*
> *decision-making process and do something con-*
> *structive. I hate myself. Why? I see myself as a*
> *failure. Why? I am 40 years old and still flounder-*
> *ing. Why? Something is not right in my life! I have*
> *killed myself. I cannot give myself freedom to*
> *laugh, to be joyful, to love or to be loved. I have*
> *spent my life trying to make "A's." "A's" would get*
> *me what and where I wanted, I thought. In this*
> *push for false legitimacy, I snuffed out my True*
> *Self. I killed myself. I want to let go of my rigidity*
> *and my need to control.*

The crash occurred on November 23, 1987, in the midst of a social work practice class. For the month prior, I had had a tenuous hold on my facade of well-being, and all my energy was channelled into simply hanging on until the end of the semester. I could feel myself becoming more frantic as finals approached, but I stuffed the wads of fear down into my stomach, telling myself I did not have time to deal with all this "stuff" right now. I had to make all "A's." Well, the Universe knew differently. Ready or not, I was going to receive what I had been asking for!

A classmate and I were sitting in the center of a horse-shoe arrangement of tables where our peers were situated. The classmate and I were facing each other, role-playing client and therapist. I was the therapist. She was my client. Our case scenario was listed in our texts which we had in our laps. I began the interview effectively but after about two questions my brain shut down. I could not make any connections. It was like a thick fog had choked off thoughts from any accessibility. A surge of panic gripped me. Think! Think! I whispered silently. Nothing. The harder I forced myself to remain calm, the more desperate I became. "You fool! You aren't competent to be a therapist! You don't know the perfect question to ask this client. There is a perfect question, you know. THE question which will cause this client to unfold to you is known by everyone in this room except you. Ha! Are you ever egotistical to think you could ever help people!" my Voice ridiculed in my head.

My professor detected my distress when I glanced into his eyes. He tried to reassure me, but I was dead meat for my Voice.

I slammed my textbook shut, the slap startling everyone in the hushed room. I exploded into tears wailing, "I can't do this. I'm a worthless failure!"

I heard my outburst but could not believe it had come from my mouth. Nor could I believe myself as I jumped up, threw my book on the table, and ran out the door. I fled into the bathroom across the hall, locked the door, and sobbed my heart out. It felt so releasing that I didn't even feel ashamed about my childish uproar of a few minutes before.

The final strands of webbing securing me to my old Self had disintegrated, leaving me shattered at the bottom of the cliff. There could now begin the arduous process of sorting: tossing out, keeping, reassembling.

Baby Steps

I quit school and decided to be totally selfish. I had the time and the financial security to take a two- or three-year focused respite. So, I entered the cave of myself and said I would not emerge until I felt whole and strong within myself. This would require almost exactly two years and a topsy-turvy ride through many emotions.

For the first four months, I experienced an engulfing tiredness. I could not hurry or push myself. I was forced to take one thing at a time. My eyelids felt incredibly heavy, as if they were going to close shut involuntarily with a screeching boom like Medieval castle doors. At times, my brain refused to think, and all I could do was sleep.

My wardrobe consisted of one gray, loose-fitting sweat outfit for day and my pajamas for night.

I read. I read anything I could get my hands on. I read anything that anyone suggested. The books, supplemented with my thinking and writing, opened an array of new perspectives. The questions I had! One day I would feel exhilarated, thinking I had found the answers, and the next day I would be confronted with a contradictory theory which blew away my smugness. There was more to this thing called life than I had ever considered.

If I were going to commit to lifelong growth, constant upheaval would now be my companion. This notion put a real snafu in my belief that life eventually reaches a comfortable plateau where no more adjustments are required. I wasn't too thrilled at the loss of this orderly philosophy.

Besides reading, I taught myself to meditate and refreshed myself on Yoga.

My new Higher Power became a formless energy field of white light I call Energy of the Universe, E.O.U. E.O.U. fits my idea of God.

I developed an interest in rebirthing. I familiarized myself with the deep breathing technique and unclogged barricaded energy which I had suppressed.

I discovered my first power animal, the wolf. I asked myself what my feminine and my masculine symbols might look like and then drew the full moon and a lush Maui mountain.

I discontinued visualizing Daddy high up in Heaven somewhere watching me, always available should I need his love or his punishment. This imagery was enslaving me rather than strengthening me. As one of my best girlfriends in Georgia rejoiced, "Yeah! Your dad is doing his own neat stuff now anyway!"

I began verbalizing, though in a limited way, feelings to my husband. If I was too reluctant to express feelings face to face, I at least wrote them or drew them on paper.

During quiet moments, I sensed a terrible longing for the seashore. The ache was sometimes physically painful. I tried to ignore it, but something about the ocean was calling me.

I realized there was a purpose for my return to Oklahoma. I had much to learn and here was where I needed to learn it. I understood now why it had not been imperative for me to connect with people and develop acquaintances. This was not to be a social season in my life. I needed to turn inward and keep my own counsel. Having no outside demands was for me, the thinker and the plodder, the ultimate umbrella of protection.

17

Solitude At My Power Spot

ONE EVENING IN THE BABY-STEP PERIOD I just described, as dusk gently melded into darkness, I sat on the patio watching one of the spectacular Oklahoma sunsets. Only I wasn't merely seeing the raspberry purples, the cotton-candy pinks, and the frosted oranges. I was becoming them. They were becoming me. I felt something inside those soft, pastel colors nourishing me, loving me, protecting me. I knew that it was feeding me. It had always been feeding me and always would. "It" was E.O.U. and it glowed in every living and nonliving thing above, on, or within the earth as well as every other body in our universe and perhaps beyond. I knew I would never be alone again. I knew I was healing, and that my wisdom and power lay in trusting my own instincts.

By the time the stars were twinkling, I felt like crying with gratitude. Warmed with the knowledge of my own beauty and value, I inhaled a deep breath and felt a liquid contentment soothe my body.

With this reaffirmation of my worth, I seriously listened to the restless nudges piped to me from the confines of my unconscious. Time alone at the beach seemed more and more necessary for my healing, but I didn't know why. On certain days, I was harried by a panicky feeling relating to the shortness of time left in my life. A trip to the beach seemed like such an extravagance. Could I afford to idle away four weeks? Could I afford not to do everything possible to promote my own well- being? NO! I would go.

After a rather fitful sleep the night of March 31, 1988, I locked myself and my bags in my VW Rabbit and headed east to a Destin, Florida, condominium I had reserved for the month of April. I was both excited and scared.

The condo and the whole month were more rewarding than I ever dreamed. I heard Dr. K's voice ringing in my head every time I started feeling guilty about this sabbatical. In his adieu he advised me, "If you don't do one thing the entire month, that is okay. You need to just assimilate the many recent unfoldings in your life. Being with yourself is all that counts."

Some people have a mystical union with another man or woman, some form of fine art, poetry, music, or God. My sense of oneness has always come with Nature, especially the ocean.

Immediately and effortlessly, I reset my system to an hourless timetable. I abandoned my wrist watch and geared all my activities to my body clock. I arose with the sun, ate breakfast, sat on the patio writing or thinking, walked on the beach, watched television, ate lunch, read frivolous novels or shopped in town, napped, walked another hour on the beach, ate supper, watched more television or read more of a book or did more writing, and then went to bed.

I strove to live in the present moments so that future ones could not haunt me. I soaked up each sound, each color, each smell, each texture, and each face.

I was looking people in the eye and smiling at them. They smiled back, too! Sometimes we even chatted and laughed uproariously. I felt caressed by those moments, and I enjoyed the loving feeling.

At the end of my first week, while browsing in a shop, I saw a little plaque with these words painted on it, "Happiness is not what you have but what you enjoy." This message shined the spotlight on my life of negativity. I had not been enjoying much of anything. I had chosen to live my life as a sourpuss. I was being given the chance to put myself together the way I wanted to be! For a few moments, I felt flushed with love for all of me — just as I was — even with my bulimia!

Reflections on my life sneaked into every activity during this month. For example, after reading six pages of a best-selling book, I would find myself thinking about my issue of power. I never had power while growing up. My desperate need for love as a child made me compliant and willing to accede my autonomy. I continued to give everyone power over me, especially my Voice. I wrote:

> *Ever since I was a tiny child, I have had not only the fear of exploding but of imploding as well. I was fearful of caving in and then crumbling and turning to dust. Fearful of just folding up one day and not existing anymore. Then in my preteens and teens I became suicidal. I actually WANTED to die, and if I lived, I never wanted to live past forty.*
>
> *Surprisingly, when these suicidal thoughts entered my head, I called upon my Voice to reinstill life in me. You see, I practiced repeating vicious, self-deprecating thoughts to myself because I actually believed I was worthless, fat, ugly, and unlovable. My Voice and my body were like a ruthless lion tamer and his prize. The Voice held the cutting whip, and my body received the blows. But like the lion, after the Voice whipped me awhile, I reared up, bared my teeth, and clawed back.*
>
> *This interchange became a daily production inside my head, and after it was over, I felt alive, renewed and driven once again. I could once more focus upon my goal and push myself mercilessly toward it. These theatrics became survival for me. I grew prouder and prouder of myself for enduring more and more painful onslaughts. My*

persecutory Voice has become as natural a part of me as my breathing or my heartbeat. I feel angry about engaging in such needless, helpless activity. I don't need to punish myself anymore. I am safe now.

Tangential to power was shame. I looked at the rules and behaviors perpetuating shame in my family. The #1 rule was: "We do not talk about feelings." I was trying to remain loyal to this family rule.

Rule #2 was: "Be in control at all times." Was this dogma ever ingrained in my personality! Lately, I noticed that as I listened and trusted my feelings, the closer I got to my True Self. The closer I got to my True Self, the louder and more judgmental my Voice became because it was losing control. It needed me to distrust my True Self so that I would remain helpless and in its fist. Challenging my Voice might be a temporary torment, but it was necessary to cross this hurdle to reach powerfulness. I had been assured that my obstinacy (not wanting to eat nutritiously, not wanting to go to art therapy, not wanting to take my medication, not wanting to keep appointments, and just plain not wanting to go anywhere) was my symbolic way of digging in against my battering Voice. Stubbornness would work itself out of my Inner Child after she had popped her firecrackers of rebellion.

While tidying up the coffee table in the condo one morning, I uncovered my "I need . . ." list. I studied it closely and asked myself if I could give myself permission to have these needs.

Turning several pages backward in my notebook, I reviewed my list of limiting beliefs. I saw how my "now-or-never" thinking bordered so closely to "all-or-nothing" thinking. Both thought patterns triggered my scarcity issues (fears of not having an adequate supply of ANYTHING) and thus a binge/purge. I formulated this affirmation to repeat whenever I felt I was running out of time, money, ideas, energy, etc.: "The E.O.U. will help me."

Beach walks provided my most fertile thinking ground. Some days I drifted into a reverie about Mother and Daddy. I had no idea what my parents were really like. All I knew were these two superhuman figures I had created in my child's mind. I had to learn to see Daddy not as an idol but as an erring human being. Then I had to let go of him. I had to let go of trying to change my mother into a paragon of devotion and to let her be who and where she was. This concept of letting go of control was especially tough for me, not just in regard to my parents, but to my husband, my friends, and myself. I so easily mistook that which my ego said was best for me as the advice of my True Self. (I had to work another year and a half to distinguish the difference.)

Other days I juggled thoughts triggered by Shakti Gawain's *Living In The Light*. My masculine aspects, which were action, directness, achievement, and assertiveness, were not balanced with my feminine aspects of intuition, feelings, and nurturing. How did these aspects tie into my bulimia, if at all? I wrote, trying to sort out thoughts:

If masculine = acting; taking charge; moving in the world. If feminine = intuition. Then I have rebuked my feminine side most of my life — clearly since the binge/purging began. I have definitely been intellectualizing since I was 22 years old, when the bulimia started.

As I remember the onset of bulimia, I feel a hardness freeze my body. My masculine side was perverted from a helpful energy to a persecutory energy. It was like a killer moved into my body — a ripping beast eating me alive from the inside out. It was bent on total control.

The first thing my Voice denied me was food. If feeling hungry = feminine impulse and getting food = masculine action, then denying my hunger was actually denying my femininity! My feminine side went into hiding. It was waiting until it felt safe to reappear. Why did my masculine side become so cruel? I trained it to be that way.

Could it also be my internalized Father? Daddy needed to dominate and control and was fearful of his feminine power. Maybe Daddy was afraid that if he listened to his feminine side he would lose his individual identity and his separateness. Daddy wanted his separateness at any cost.

Through bulimia, I achieved separateness through all its costs. My bulimia was my way of indirectly expressing my power through manipulation, that is manipulating through sickness. All these years, bulimia, under the arm of my warped male energy, was trying to keep me separated from my female energy.

One afternoon, a squadron of pelicans soared overhead and I counted exactly twelve. I wondered if the group was paired and if they were six couples scouting for an overnight nesting spot. Couples. Love. Marriage. Marriages, past and present, filed through my head. I made mistakes. My husbands made mistakes. There was so much to marriage I had yet to learn. So much about my divorce I had yet to grieve. So many feelings surrounding it were left unresolved. Would the pain ever go away?

On warm, sunny days, bathers and beachcombers donned swim suits. I finally broke down and slipped into my faded, baggy, one-piece suit for my morning hike on the sand. Of course, I took inventory of my body before walking out the door. I decided I really loved my body and wouldn't want to be anyone else but me. I would never be 20 years old again, but at 20 I was neither thin nor happy. With proper nutrition, I knew the scaly skin patches on my face would disappear, and the mild bloating in my abdomen would subside once my body regulated to three suitable meals a day. My menstrual cycle was occurring regularly now, and I was proud and grateful for it. I couldn't mend the tiny broken capillaries on my face, chest, and abdomen, but I could keep practicing relaxation to relieve my stress.

The main casualty in this war with bulimia was my teeth. They were irreparably damaged. My once strong, white, and solid teeth were now yellow shells. Most of my bottom teeth have composite fillings on the outside surfaces because the enamel has been gouged away by the hydrochloric acid regurgitated with food during a purge. The rest of my teeth look like old, worn mountains, chipped and cracked by ruthless winds and water. But with the support of caring dentists, like Dr. Miller in Columbus and Dr. Eliot in Edmond, my teeth and I received loving care. Dr. Eliot was genuinely interested in my struggle, and he listened with his heart. His pats on my shoulder at the conclusion of every visit conveyed his encouragement. If there is one thing a person in recovery requires, it is encouragement!

One decision I reached concretely during this month, but after great turmoil, was the fact that I wanted a wise female therapist. I was ready to face some gentle confrontation from a self-assured yet loving woman. All of my therapists had been men. Through them I learned about masculine power which was forceful without being verbally, emotionally, or physically abusive. Now I wanted to learn about developing my feminine power.

Good times fly away so quickly. My peaceful hiatus came to an end, and I had not written one word of poetry or sketched one drawing. There were only thirteen days out of the thirty that I did not binge/purge. A few days were spent shedding tears. Several days I chugged through with my mind on neutral. But throughout, I had just "BEEN." I had felt no pressure to "BE" or "DO" anything. Naturally, I wanted this relaxed existence to coast on and on, but the real world awaited me.

Had I known the pain ahead, I would have stayed secluded in Destin. Had I known the bliss ahead, I would have taken the fastest plane back to Oklahoma. I am thankful I did not know either facet of the growth before me.

18

"Coping" Does Not Mean "Not Feeling"

MY MOOD NOSE-DIVED IN MAY. I felt trapped in a wasteland. Nothing eased my pain — not even crying, bingeing and purging, or talking.

I terminated with Dr. K and began sessions with a therapist named Martha Baldwin. I chose her purely on a gut feeling I had after watching her on local television one night. What she said really rocked my socks. It was as if she had tapped into my brain and heard every anguishing question.

I knew by the time I touched her office door handle I was in a loving place. The walkway up to the reconverted house was enclosed with a cool arbor of vines and flowers. Under a trellis woven with wisteria was a wooden deck with wrought-iron park benches and a porch swing. Upon entering her sitting room, I spotted the huge bulletin board filled with groups, workshops, seminars, books, tapes, and pictures. Green plants adorned the waiting room. A lump clogged my throat. I moved to a chair, sat down, and tears filled my eyes. I had found an oasis! I felt so safe.

Talking with Martha was easy. She zeroed in on my childhood issues. She said we would work on teaching me how to establish a relationship with my Inner Child and thus open communication with my pockets of pain. She also wanted me to take a committed look at possible sexual abuse in my family. (Here was this topic again!)

I felt very happy when I left her office. This trusting oneself really paid off!

For every celebration, though, there was hell to pay from my Voice. It lambasted me like a crazed hoodlum and left me battered in its pillage. It wanted no creativity, no fun, no success, no daydreaming, no nurturing. Weariness buried me. As I progressed in my journey of self-discovery, I thought the path would become clearer. Instead of clarity, I bumped into more questions and more feelings. I wasn't so sure I wanted to continue on this road!

Martha was sensitive to my reluctance and fear, but she did not let me flop around in a victim dance. She knew I was willing to work, so she demanded action. I would have to use my body if I were going to work with her. And I do believe it was the body work in conjunction with the mental work which finally set me free.

Martha doesn't ask things of her clients which she has not done or does not do herself, so I trusted her. She knew what I was going through, and she knew it was tough. She was gentle when I needed gentleness. She was truthful when I didn't want to face the truth. She praised me when I needed praising. She believed in me when I didn't believe in me. She stood behind me while I rebuilt my new Self, always coaching, "You can do it! Keep breathing!"

For starters, she frequently urged me to hit a chair for about a minute with her bataca. A bataca is a sponge bat which is used to hit inanimate objects or other people, thus helping patients unlock feelings. I felt so ridiculous and mechanical at first, until one day I overflowed with tears. I didn't know exactly from where the tears originated, but shedding them was a great relief. Once I had opened the channel to this rawness, feelings poured out with the help of several therapeutic techniques.

Rage was my predominant emotion, and it necessitated physical discharges. Walking, crying, beating my orange pillow, and rebirthing had served me well on a piecemeal basis. I had never been consistent in using any of those devices because after unleashing feelings I was nagged with guilt about betraying the "be-in-control-at-all-times" rule. I was also terrified that I might be destroyed by rage if I ever acknowledged the massiveness of it.

Martha reassured me that my unconscious would not gush forth in one swift torrent sweeping me into uncontrollable madness. With her guarantee, I devised my homemade version of a bataca and began daily physical workouts.

I confiscated Doug's six-foot souvenir bullwhip, stuffed plugs into my ears, and started whipping the garage floor. Along with the physical raising and lowering of my right arm, the cracking noise of the tip of the bullwhip against the unpliable concrete was extremely gratifying. I felt energy flowing down my arm and out my fingers.

Expressing rage for rage's sake was missing the point, though. It wasn't until the morning that Doug made an observation of my helpless behavior that I connected my rage with my wounded Inner Child.

After he left for work, I was burning with hurt and anger, dueling with the Voice about whether or not to binge/purge. Then I remembered my bullwhip. I lifted it from its wooden pegs on the coat rack and slapped it ferociously against the seasoned garage floor. I spat out my hate to everyone in general, "I hate you! I hate you!" After about twenty-five minutes, I dropped the whip and sank into a ball, crying like the devastated child I had been 38 years ago.

Once I proved the value of this exercise to my own healing, I became more creative in using it. If my rage were directed at a specific person, I visualized that person's face on the pavement and spoke my unedited feelings with each strike of the whip. The freeing thing about this entire exercise was that whatever I said was uncensored and unheard by anyone but myself. I could be as irrational and spiteful as I had ever wanted to be and no one would be hurt.

Later, as I came to know Little Suzy better, I would reserve my left arm for her cathartic work. My right arm handled my Present Adult's feelings.

During "dead pattern" episodes when I was completely blocking all emotions, I resorted to a chant while I hit the concrete. I repeated out loud, "I release my rage. I release my guilt. I release my shame. I release my fear. Up and out. Out. Out. I release my rage from every cell in my body. I release my guilt from every cell in my body, etc." Then I would voice affirmations such as, "I refuse to be a victim. I am healthy and whole. I am safe." Many times I avoided a binge/purge by rotely pushing myself through this routine.

Grief and sadness were extricated through Gestalt episodes and letter writing. Daddy had died with reams of material left unsaid or unfinished between us, and I felt a tormenting lack of closure with him. Four years after his death, I tried to reconcile my hurt by visiting his grave and talking to him. I missed Daddy frightfully and told him so in that tearful soliloquy.

Now, ten years after his death, my sorrow was blending with my anger and fear. By pretending he was comfortable in the stuffed chair in my study while I was poised on its accompanying footstool, I rattled on with whatever felt important for me to say. Sometimes, my Present Adult communicated with his Adult. Other times, Little Suzy communicated with his Adult. One time, I even had an eerie feeling he had been present and understood. Whether he had been or not doesn't matter. What does matter is that through these conversations I disengaged from some of the poisonous hooks that polluted our relationship.

Writing letters was most beneficial in helping Little Suzy mourn Joe Ben's death. She wrote him a remarkable letter and when she signed it, "Your sister, Suzy," the pen froze in my hand. That was the first time I ever addressed myself to him as his sister. Joe Ben became flesh and blood at that instant, and my Present Adult sensed the incredible pustule of feelings and memories festering within Little Suzy concerning his loss.

Expressing my feelings by writing and drawing with my nondominant hand, which is my left, was a real eye-opener for someone like me who is right-hand dominant. Our left brain is verbal, analytical, linear, and temporal. In other words, it deals with thinking. It controls the right side of our body. Our right brain deals with feeling and is nonverbal, spatial, nontemporal, and sees things as wholes. The right brain controls the left side of our body. Hence, when I write and draw with my left hand, I suspend all criticism and logic so that anything I put down on paper is spontaneous and unedited.

From Lucia Capacchione's *The Power of Your Other Hand*, I learned I could use my left hand to dialogue not only with the various parts of my personality, such as Little Suzy, the Voice, and Present Adult, but with ailing parts of my body as well. For instance, when my right hand wrote and asked my pounding headache, "Who or what are you?," my left hand succinctly responded with this fiery volley, "I am your adventurous, risk-taking adult. Let me out of here!"

When words could not answer "Who or what are you?," I would let my left hand scribble a picture as a reply. The information I could receive was remarkable.

Like the nondominant writing and drawing, my dreams allowed rich, unconscious material to filter to the surface. During the summer of 1988, I "found" Dr. Carl Jung, and his books, including ones on dreams, were tremendous mental nourishment for me. His essence seemed to float out of his words and surround me as I read. He asked some of the same questions I was asking. His mind thrilled me, and I knew I had found a great teacher from the past.

It was he who kindled my interest in dreams. I collected notes on different dream symbols and began analyzing each of my dreams. I discovered my recurring dream about my high school heartthrob was a message to deal with my sexuality. In the dream, I was one face among hundreds in a crowd of women. I tried urgently to catch this boy's attention by yelling his name and waving my arms. I just wanted him to look at me and say hello, but he always walked past, ignoring me. My spider nightmare was encouraging me to deal with my ensnarement with Mother.

After I initiated rolfing sessions, my dreaming burst into flower. Color dreams, which I had rarely, became commonplace. Themes of being murdered and sexually abused were replayed several times a week. It was not unusual for me to awaken and find myself crying or flailing my arms. Inspiring and loving dreams also were painted with the brushes belonging to my deepest artist. Sleep is the only time I give up controlling myself so this was a prime time which my Higher Self used quite efficiently to speak to me.

Observing elaborate pictures in my dreams and being responsible for creating my own images during waking hours were two different propositions. When Martha dangled imagery as a tool for recalling repressed memories, I practically laughed in her face. Indeed, I do believe the Inner Child in each of us holds all the early memories and feelings which color our lives forever, but how would I know that what I remembered wasn't just my imagination? Martha said matter-of-factly, "Trust yourself."

When Martha asked me to conjure up an image of Little Suzy, I could produce nothing except a flat, black-and-white, cardboard projection. We kept trying and I refused to give up. I had heard and read about others' successes with imagery and was determined to develop this skill in myself.

Mother complied with my request to mail me some of my childhood pictures. As I gazed at my sweet, beautiful, little face, I began to establish an ardent love for this part of me. In a way, I had a child now. I had a child of my very own, and I could appreciate in a small way what it must feel like to be a mother. Tenderness toward myself took on a whole new meaning. I became the giver as well as the receiver.

Daily relaxation periods of one-half to one hour ensued, during which I closed my eyes, called forth Little Suzy's image, and asked her how she was feeling. She took it from there.

Early on in my ignorance, I presumed Little Suzy would give me all the answers the minute I called her with open arms, proffering love. What a foolish assumption! Children are much more astute than we give them credit for. Little Suzy needed my love, but she demanded my respect, my complete honesty, and my pledge to safeguard her welfare. The gap between us would be bridged according to her schedule. No chicanery or shortcuts. I had disavowed her existence many years ago, and she was not going to sail back into my life on hollow promises.

Above all else, Little Suzy needed safety if I were to get to know her. She did not trust me in the beginning and would not even allow me to touch her. She needed a place where she could say and do and think whatever she needed or wanted. If she needed to scream her lungs out, she could. If she needed to stomp her feet, she could. If she wanted to smear her finger-paints on the wall, rip apart a storybook, or cuddle her teddy bear while rocking, she could.

We conferred about a playroom on the beach. She was ecstatic. I drew a blueprint for her playroom, built it, and furnished it all in my mind. It contained: bookshelves lined with books; a miniature desk; an art table piled with paper and crayolas, modeling clay, finger-paints, watercolors, and pastels; a sandbox; a slide; stuffed animals; a doll house; a record player with records; and two rocking chairs, one for me and one draped with a cozy, blue blanket for her.

When Little Suzy entered it for the first time, she clasped her chubby fingers together and bounced up and down on her tiptoes. She said she loved me and she loved her playroom.

I blessed the playroom with Love and Light, reminding Little Suzy that nothing and no one could ever harm her while she was in this room. It was a magical room. No hurricane could ever demolish it. The sun shone into every window every day, and the moon beamed in at night.

Objects broken, thrown around, or spilled would return to original form and place after each temper tantrum.

For the first few weeks, I joined Little Suzy in the sandbox. I slipped in probing questions between the pressing out of sand castles. The inquisitions made her withdraw so I honored her privacy and her need for pure play.

She laughed and chattered away like a chipmunk. She had such vitality and joy, but she was incredibly lonely and afraid.

Soon, in my visions, she was curling under the crook of my arm in my rocking chair while I read or sang to her. She soaked up the love like a giant sponge.

Little Suzy acted very cool to me when I checked in on days after bingeing and purging. I knew my bulimia was abusive to her. It was rejection in her eyes. It was also confusing to her. I had promised to protect her, and bingeing/purging was hypocritical behavior. I let the Voice flatten us both.

One day I remember feeling abominable about a binge/purge. I had tried doggedly to resist. When time came for my daily imagery with Little Suzy, she met me with fear and hostility in her eyes. I began crying in real life and verbalized all my feelings of self-disgust and worthlessness. This little child and I came into full view in my mind, and her wee arms wrapped around my neck while her rabbit-smooth cheek pressed against mine for about five seconds. She then leaned back and looked into my eyes and said, "I love you. I trust you. You are working to be real."

From that point forward, she became an active participant in my life, and not a day goes by that I am not aware that Little Suzy is present, celebrating or needing attention. When I hum to myself, dress in lively colored clothes, dance, play chase with my dog, treat myself to a chocolate chip cookie, or paint a picture, I know Little Suzy is hurrahing. When I experience that unquenchable hunger, the "dead pattern," the wild rebellion, hyperventilation, middle-of-the-night nausea, irrational fear of being touched, reluctance to part with my teddy bear, or dread at seeing the sun set, I know that behind the symptom is a painful childhood memory. I stop, illuminate a halo of Love and Light around Little Suzy's image, and ask her what is happening.

Just as my Inner Child is a part of my make-up, so is my Voice. Unlike my Inner Child, though, I wanted to reject this seemingly negative part of me. Martha confronted me one day with my own oft-repeated plea, "I want to love all of me." "If you genuinely want to love all of yourself, Susan, you are going to have to quit fighting your Voice. Why don't you try sending it Love and Light the next time it trounces you?" she hinted.

I would never have believed how needy my Voice was for love until I felt it grabbing and clinging to each phosphorescent word of tenderness. By loving my Voice and understanding that it was conditioned to react with cruelty, it has become less ill- tempered and more low-keyed.

Along with my bullwhip energy releases, the Gestalt exercises, the letter writing, the nondominant hand writing and drawing, dream analysis, rolfing, and imagery, I used pure gut courage in my healing process. In fact, it was all I had one day when I decided to ride out one of my panic attacks.

This symptom was the most terrifying of all for me, because when I was sucked into this tornadic eddy, I felt like my head was going to explode. I lost my capacity to think, to use my knowledge, to reason. Any fragmented thoughts I might have raced in a circular motion with no punctuation indicating a beginning or an end. I lost control, and insanity or death felt like the only two escapes.

This particular afternoon, I stretched out on the floor of my study to meditate. Just as I was centering in the energy of my heart, I felt that spiral of fear growing from a pinpoint in the middle of my head into a full-fledged rampage. I kept breathing and for some reason decided this would be the last panic attack I would ever shun! I was tired of being tyrannized by this fear and wanted to know what was on the other side of it. I was prepared to die.

As the pinwheel of spinning expanded, I felt nauseated. "Oh, my! I'm going to vomit all over myself!" I thought. "Well, I give myself permission. I will clean it up after this is over if I'm still alive." The nausea faded away.

Rearing out of my mind leapt this next horrific thought, "My head is going to burst wide open! Doug is going to come home from work and find my brains spewed all over the floor and walls! I'm going to die right here!"

Then, calmly, another voice stated, "So be it. I do not want to live chained to these panic attacks. At least I will die valiantly."

The sound of a rushing wind with a muffled buzz inside it drenched my mind. It felt like gravity was pulling my head one way and my body the opposite way. I wanted to black out because the terror was so intense, but I forced myself to stay present.

"I must walk into this. I must become this energy. It is only energy," I heard a voice think.

So I quit pushing the energy away, filled a deep breath with the forceful waves, and pulled them down through my neck and shoulders into my chest. Like a flood, this energy gushed into every other part of my body down to my toes.

The spinning ceased, but my body was vibrating and felt like it had no physical boundaries. Next I noticed a sensual awakening in my abdomen. It scared and confused me, but this was not the time to analyze it. It danced around awhile and melted into the larger overall energy field which, in turn, evaporated from my body.

I opened my eyes. I was still alive. I had one less demon to contend with! My smile was so big it could have wrapped around the equator.

As incredible as it may sound, the strides I made during these ten months didn't elevate my self-esteem. While muddling through the ups and downs, I more often than not felt bogged down. I continued to count my failures and to focus on my nonproductivity. Especially discouraging to me was the persistent bulimia. In March, 1989, I made a list of every tactic I had ever used to usurp the compulsion:

1. Cognitive therapy
2. Medication
3. Diuretics
4. Keeping a journal of feelings
5. Keeping a journal of every bite consumed
6. Stocking my kitchen shelves with goodies
7. Removing all goodies from my kitchen shelves
8. Not carrying money in my purse to eliminate impulse buying
9. Chewing food and spitting it out before swallowing
10. Preparing a healthy, three-meal-per-day food plan
11. Banishing the word "diet" from my vocabulary
12. Substituting an alternative activity, such as tennis, walking, bike riding, dancing, reading, going to a movie, going to a museum or art gallery, or doing housework every time I felt the urge to binge/purge
13. Calling someone to get a verbal hug
14. Twelve-step programs
15. Joining an eating disorders support group
16. Delaying a binge/purge for two to three hours
17. Video taping a binge and a purge
18. Chewing a stick of gum when I wanted to binge/purge
19. Repeating affirmations daily
20. Meditating after each meal and feeling my feelings
21. Somatic releases of feelings, such as screaming, pounding my orange pillow, or hitting with my bullwhip
22. Rebirthing myself

23. Reading a morning meditation
24. Playing my own cassette tape of favorite affirmations daily
25. Writing a daily affirmation or inspiring quote on my erasable marker board
26. Breaking my day into three smaller segments of 6:00 a.m.-12:00 noon, 12:00 noon-5:00 p.m., and 5:00 p.m.-10:00 p.m., trying to abstain only for the length of each segment
27. Art therapy
28. Writing with my nondominant hand

Willpower was never going to eradicate my eating disorder. Dr. Felker was right when he said my bulimia might be the last symptom of all to fall away.

Obviously I had more digging to do.

19

Gifts! Gifts! Gifts!

NOVEMBER, 1989, FOUND ME ONCE MORE at the condominium in Destin, Florida. Though a belated birthday present to myself, it had been reserved since July. With 1990 to be consumed with sprucing up and selling the house and eventually moving, I felt there might not be another chance to take a big lump of time away from Edmond. Also, I was signed up for a weekend retreat in mid-November at Pine Mountain, Georgia.

After partially unpacking about 3:30 p.m. on Friday, November 3, I scurried to the beach for a short walk and to watch the sunset. Walking didn't seem to soothe me, so I sat down, scooted my derriere on the sand, and made a roost for myself like an old, fat hen. My back was upright, my legs bent with my knees against my chest, and my arms crisscrossed on top of my knees.

I did not feel happy! The water was navy blue in color and as smooth as a small lake undisturbed because of no wind. Where were the crashing waves and the foaming surf? Where were my butterflies of excitement? Where were the superlatives that usually poured from my mouth to describe the beauty of this place? WHERE was the connection, like a surge of electricity, linking my soul to the ancient, everpresent power of the ocean?

I sat there frustrated and extremely disappointed! I felt like I was choking on some awareness trying to surface.

"Just calm down and be patient," my Nurturing Adult said.

"But this is not the reaction I've been dreaming about for three months! I thought I would feel so peaceful and excited to be back!" my Present Adult retorted. "What's the matter? What's so different since I was here last?"

I flopped backwards onto the icy beach, stretched my arms outward, and grabbed a fistful of sand in each hand.

"What's so different? Look at what has happened to you since then! Remember all the peak experiences? My, gosh! Give yourself credit for some incredible work!" Nurturing Adult exclaimed.

I propelled myself upright again.

"You're right! I have been transformed! My viewpoints, my perspectives, even sometimes I think my molecular make-up itself, have been altered," Present Adult mused.

My mind flashed over each peak experience, and I was in awe of my growth.

Peak Experience #1

LITTLE SUZY CRIES OUT

The prelude to this experience began in April, 1989, while I was questioning everything. Like rocks in a polishing tumbler, questions bumped in my head:

> *Is my Voice the disowned part of my Inner Child? Did I split off from this part that felt bad, worthless, lazy, fat, and stupid and deny its presence? Has Little Suzy adopted this Voice as a tactic to get my attention so that I will notice her feelings? Or is my Voice my disowned Shadow Side, which houses my cruelty, my self-destructiveness, my hostile aggressiveness, my selfishness, my judgmentalness, my rebelliousness, and my fear? Or is my Voice my internalized Father? Could my bulimia be a symptom of an unconscious belief*

that I deserve to be dead instead of Joe Ben? What was I to learn from Joe Ben's death? Why do I have this intense disavowal of my sexual feelings? Why are they so shameful to me? Does Willie hate me? Does Doug really love me? Do I really love Doug? Or are we clinging to each other in an attempt to hide from ourselves? Do I want to trust Doug? Why do I shrink from initiative, assertiveness, directness, and creativity? Am I courageous enough to act on what I believe in? What am I not listening to or not paying attention to? Am I prepared to commit myself to my individual purpose in life? Can I let go and say, "Thy will be done?" Why is my ego so attached to polarities of good/evil, right/wrong, all/nothing?

I was reminded once more that all my history since my birth did have a purpose — a guiding hand. "It" had led me to this point right NOW. Inscribed in the Master Plan was my return to Oklahoma at a critical juncture in my life, my 40th birthday, so that I could be reborn. My lifelong premonition that I would die at age 40 had been true, except that my death had been psychological, not physical.

From all these soundings, there came one clear decision which was to open me once and for all. I wrote on April 4, 1989:

The time has come to delve into my three-year-old's terror. Maybe that's the reason for my insatiable hunger the past two weeks. I must feel Little Suzy's terror. NOW is the time. I give myself permission to cry and to feel.

Of course, when the crack appeared one month later, I was caught off guard. It was my regular Monday night therapy group, and Martha spontaneously suggested that we have a group rebirthing for those who wanted to participate. Jim, our experienced rebirthing facilitator, was randomly assigned to me. He was my gift for this evening.

I lay on my back and initiated my deep breathing. I was aware of others' voices and drifted back and forth between their sounds and my thoughts. This continued for what seemed like an hour, and I didn't feel I was penetrating the nucleus of my energy. I was about to give up when I detected an aching grief — a sorrow — and only screaming seemed to be the answer.

I began to wail like a little baby, and my hands were all curled up and my arms writhing like an infant's. The sorrow was a big pool. The screams came from deep within that pool. I felt decompressed as they pumped out.

Then I started crying. I cried and cried. I needed to speak. Jim said, "Say whatever you need to say." I cried, "I'm so sorry, Joe Ben. I'm so sorry you died. I'm so sorry." I repeated my lament several times.

The crying stopped momentarily but began again. I pictured my Nurturing Adult comforting Little Suzy. She told my Inner Child how much she loved her. Then I felt the tears and the pain ebb away.

I opened my eyes and thanked Jim effusively. I reached a pocket of pain I had been trying to reach and release all my life, and it came so unexpectedly! I felt very, very peaceful.

Peak Experience #2

MADAME COLORFUL

This experience was preceded by two events: (1) Gilda Radner's death, and (2) Shirley MacLaine's story in *Going Within* about a friend of hers who had AIDS.

I had eaten Sunday morning breakfast at the corner fast-food restaurant and was leisurely thumbing through the newspaper when I found the article announcing Gilda Radner's death. A lump swelled in my chest. I felt tears in my eyes. I had to get out of that restaurant. I scooped up my paper, forgot my coffee, went back to retrieve it, and as I was hurriedly trying to get out the side door to get to my car before I burst into tears, I dropped my coffee cup, and coffee splashed everywhere. I reported my mess and fled. I cried all the way home.

Gilda Radner was 42 years old when she died. I was currently 41 years old. I had always appreciated and enjoyed Gilda's tremendous talent, and suddenly she was gone — poof! Her existence was over and she was only 42! I felt sad, angry, and scared.

Her death stirred up my awareness of my own mortality. It made me re-examine my life. My obsessions with food and weight were such pointless wastes of energy. I was so critical of myself. I was lonely. I wanted to be involved but lacked motivation and direction.

Shirley MacLaine's friend taught her that we need to love ourselves as well as to let in the love that others give us. I had made countless lists of ways to nurture myself, but were they actually ways to love myself — my True Self? The fact that I had not made one acquaintance, much less one friend, during this Oklahoma residency testified to my pattern of keeping people at a distance.

Loving myself was at the crux of both these events, so what better way to introduce me to my True Self than through a dream:

I was visiting a very eccentric, elderly lady writing teacher at her home. She was taking me under her tutelage. She was very excited about my writing talent and was encouraging my growth. She loved me very much, and I loved her in return.

She was a fascinating woman with an array of artistic abilities that included painting, dancing, acting, and piano playing. She delighted in things mystical, but her factual knowledge was very extensive. Her personality was exuberant, energetic, childlike, flamboyant, independent, loving, generous, and assertive. She was dressed like a gypsy in a full, ankle- length skirt of handwoven, multicolored threads with a matching bulky, long-sleeved blouse. Surrounding her thinning brown hair was an exquisite silk turban.

With a smile on her face and her hands waving through the air in an expansive gesture, she invited me to join her for dinner that night. She wanted to continue our in-depth discussion about philosophy and life.

I declined, saying I had to study. In truth, I did not want to go.

In her voluminous voice, she delivered her benign ultimatum, "Nonsense! It is Friday night and that is our night for fun. I will meet you at the restaurant."

She faded into the bookshelves lining her library where we were talking, and I secretly felt excited about our appointment.

When I awoke from this dream, I had the most wonderful glow of bliss. This creative lady was my True Self, and I named her Madame Colorful.

Peak Experience #3

A DOUBLE MIRACLE

The day after meeting Madame Colorful, I had this profound experience which jolted me so powerfully that even months later, it makes me tremble.

My odyssey began when I took our Miniature Schnauzer to the veterinarian late one afternoon for boarding during the Memorial Day weekend. I didn't want to say good-bye to Pumpkin, and she apparently didn't want to let me go either. She jumped back into the car twice while I was trying to collect all her stuff from the back seat. The second time, she leaped into the driver's seat and hunched up. When I reached for her, she bared her teeth. This was so unlike her. I knew she was frightened.

When I finally collected her, she clung to me, stiff and trembling, with one paw on each of my shoulders like a scared child. My heart was torn apart. I wanted to start crying. Abandonment issues from my childhood were being ignited.

I delivered Pumpkin to the doctor, my legs melting beneath me. I hastened out of the clinic and practiced deep breathing all the way home. I felt a mountain of sorrow and loneliness inside my chest and gut.

Recklessly, I zoomed the car into the garage once I got home, scrambled into the house, and collapsed on the bedroom floor. Guilt was eating me alive. I felt like a hard-hearted parent who had just dumped its child at the hospital and then walked out, leaving the little one to fend for itself.

I tried to calm myself by lying flat on my back with my arms at my sides and inhaling and exhaling deeply into and out of my abdomen. I needed to cry, so I let myself cry. Did I ever sob for one solid hour!

Crying opened a conduit to an abscess, and I heard myself think imperatively, "I must scream."

I moved into the guest bedroom where I knew no one would hear me. I sat on the floor, noticing the child's heirloom rocker with my old stuffed monkey and Raggedy Anne doll on its cushion. Instantly, I felt a shift in my consciousness, and I became Little Suzy. She wanted to hold Turquoise, my Present Adult's stuffed bear. I sprang up and fetched Turquoise from the chair in my study like an eagle swooping up precious prey in its talons.

Back in the guest room, I wilted on the floor and like a flash flood, tears and screams gushed out of my body. I have never felt such terror and such incredible, lacerating pain — wave after wave after wave!

Clasping the metal leg of the bed, I cried, "No! No! Please don't leave me! Don't leave me alone!" My face dropped into the carpet, and I could feel my tears dripping into the pile.

For some reason, I needed something else to hang on to, so I grabbed the wooden leg of the bedside table. A picture flashed into my mind, only for a second, but long enough to rip me apart inside. I was at the veterinarian's office. I was locked behind the bars of a cage instead of Pumpkin. Abandonment feelings wracked my body. The original wound was now completely opened.

Little Suzy wailed over and over, "Please, don't leave me! Everything is so black, and I am so scared. So scared. No!

Ben, please come back! Please! Please don't leave! No! No! Daddy, don't leave me. If you leave me, I am all alone. Please! No! Please! I can't survive!"

These pleadings went on and on until Little Suzy was gutted. My Present Adult slowly moved in and presided over my mind. Bewildered, I looked around me as if I had emerged from a time machine. Turquoise's paw was squashed flat against her tummy. Her right ear was soaked with tears and nasal fluid. Present Adult spoke to Little Suzy, "You need to be held. I need to be held. I feel helpless to give you any power. I feel paralyzed."

I lay on the floor awhile, making sure I was still intact. Rocking in a rocking chair was what I wanted. That would help! I walked into the bedroom across the hall where my big rocking chair was seated against the wall. Wedged partly under one leg of the chair was Pumpkin's white sleeping blanket. Gently, I picked it up and wrapped Turquoise like a live baby in its soft folds. I sat in the rocker. As I glanced about the room, I saw Pumpkin's green cap which Doug gave her to play with. Another wave of pain convulsed my heart. I rose, picked up the cap, tucked it into the blanket with Turquoise, and sat back down to rock. My Nurturing Adult cooed to Present Adult and Little Suzy, "I will give you both all the love, light, and power I have."

I rocked for I don't know how long saying prayers, sending loving energy to myself, and finally saying out loud, "I need a whole lot of love right now. I need a mother to hold me. I need someone to physically hold me. But there is no one. Wait. I do have Madame Colorful. Yes, of course!"

Mentally I contacted her, and she was there just as loving and caring as in my dream. How she consoled me! Her gentle strength restored some of my internal power.

When I felt resuscitated, I invited Ben and Daddy to join Madame Colorful and let me feel their love. Ben responded but Daddy never came. I understood and accepted Daddy's unavailability.

Minutes passed as I languished in the soft glow of love from my Higher Self and my brother. Then I heard a voice, which was mine, speaking in my head, but the words were not germinating from my brain. Someone was talking to me using my voice, but the thoughts belonged to this someone. I tried to still my racing heart and concentrate. It was a male entity — not a child and not an elder. Don't ask me how I knew, but after being sparked by a barb of recognition, I knew it was Ben. He communed with me, "I am sorry that what you just went through caused you to feel so much pain and fear, but you had to be opened. You had to be agape for this moment. I have been beside you all your life, you know that, don't you?"

"Yes, I've known — at least, I think I've known," I acknowledged haltingly.

"Why do you think you kept asking 'Why?' all your life? It was to keep you searching so that I could bore through to you," he explained.

"Why did you have to die?" I blurted out.

"My life was ordained to be brief so that I could help you in the most complete way possible. You see, Suzy, I took the form of your brother, but I am really one of your Teachers. I am one of the Ones who guides you in your personal growth," he answered.

I heard myself gasp out loud. Was I losing my marbles? Was I playing some fantastic trick on myself to try to explain away my life's struggle with Joe Ben's death? I inquired further, "What about Joan? She suffered immeasurably with your death, too."

"Do not concern yourself with Joan's path. Know that she is being taken care of by her own loving spirits. I am here for you," Joe Ben assured me affectionately.

I wanted to cry out with such intense feelings of gratitude and love. "What can I do to repay you? How can I express my gratitude?" I questioned.

"Take note of how you feel right now. You feel more loved than you ever have in your whole life. You trusted yourself when I appeared to you and you let me in. You accepted my love. Every day hence open yourself to love from others as well as loving yourself! Let your trust blossom," he replied.

Feeling his energy depart, I started crying. Three hours ago, I unknowingly embarked upon a journey into a mysterious realm. I had no concrete proof of its existence. All I knew for sure was that I was changed, and I now believed in miracles.

Peak Experience #4

RELIVING THE TRAUMA

The awareness that this was a peak experience hit me only after it was over. The denouement from the accident lasted seven days. I would never again doubt the authenticity of the premise that memories are stored as emotions that involve physiological responses and that can lead to physical symptoms. Let me begin by relating the alarming spill which served as my wake-up call.

It was a drizzly Sunday morning that July 23, 1989. Doug had backed out of the garage and driven off to work. The coffee was perking, and I was thrilled with the delicious opportunity to enjoy a leisurely breakfast with the thick Sunday newspaper. Not bothering to slip on shoes, I dashed to the end of the driveway to retrieve the paper, hoping I wouldn't get too wet. Once in the delicate mist, though, I felt like a little girl again. A giggle bubbled out of my mouth, and I wanted to perform a silly, carefree jig.

"Come on out and play," I yelled to Pumpkin, who observed me from the dry garage. When she declined, I snatched the newspaper and ran full speed back to shelter. My forward steps must have ceased when I re-entered the garage, because my feet slid right out from under me, and I slammed down hard on my back on that unsparing concrete! I lay there about a minute, stunned, not knowing whether to cry or to laugh. Then I felt scared.

What if I've broken some bones? What if I've broken my back? Terror gripped my mind as I pictured myself as a paraplegic. I decided I wouldn't move for awhile so that I could have time to pull myself together. Then I felt angry. Why was I going through another hairy experience all by myself? Why is Doug always gone when these things happen to me?

I moaned to Pumpkin. Talking to anything was reassuring. She licked my mouth as if to offer some consolation. I had to know the shape my back was in, so I wiggled my arms and hands. They moved! Encouraged, I wiggled my toes and then moved my legs. They moved, too! I said a prayer of thanksgiving and raised myself very, very slowly. Dizziness and nausea billowed in my system.

With choppy steps, I proceeded back to the bedroom where I reclined on the bed and rested for forty minutes. My right elbow throbbed the rest of the day, and dull, intermittent pains punched me occasionally between my shoulders and above my coccyx.

An examination later revealed only a soft tissue injury with no cracked or broken bones. My guardian angels were definitely protecting me that Sunday. And why shouldn't they have been! It was the thirty-ninth anniversary of Joe Ben's death.

The following Wednesday, Doug departed for a five-day business trip, and my usual panic feelings over abandonment were sharper than ever before, even after rehearsing all my self-help techniques. I didn't feel one whit safer. In fact, I seemed to be super sensitive to helplessness and vulnerability. Since Monday I had been too terrified to leave the house, and Turquoise was in my arms at all times. My appetite became absolutely gargantuan, and I could not get enough to eat. The feeling of being adrift and alone haunted me. What was going on?

That night, while pacing from one end of the house to the other, I stopped in the living room. The spacious silence pulled me into its bosom. I plopped down on the Tunisian rug to savor the serenity which had descended upon me.

Closing my eyes, I began meditating. Little Suzy was right there. She was in a full-fledged panic. She kept asking, "Where is Joe Ben?" She was worried about Mother and Daddy. Her world had been turned upside down, and she did not understand what was happening.

Identifying with this Inner Child, I started crying. I cried for one-and-a-half hours.

When my tears had dwindled, the significance of my fall and subsequent feelings became clear to me. My Present Adult body was inhabited by my Inner Child, and I was replaying her reactions to Joe Ben's death thirty-nine years ago that week. A healing gift was being given to me in that this time I could act as the nurturing, unconditionally loving parent and heal my Inner Child, and thus myself!

For the rest of the week, I enveloped Little Suzy in love and tolerance. I ate whatever she wanted, I cried whenever she needed, and I held her whenever she asked. It was a special interlude and jelled our relationship forever.

Peak Experience #5

AN ALBUQUERQUE MOON

During June and July of 1989, I was enrolled in a ceramics course which was very difficult for me. Not only was handling the clay a challenge, but also handling "father" issues which my teacher activated within me.

At the end of June, Martha commented that watching my deterioration the past three weeks had been like watching me die. That is exactly what had been happening. As Little Suzy's vigor withered during her continued re-experiencing of events after Joe Ben's death, my Present Adult shriveled with her.

Somehow my needs were not being met, and I was muddled about whether I was still on my true heart's path. After meditating one day, the message was clear that I was to travel to workshops, retreats, and seminars in order to learn some valuable lessons about myself.

Brugh Joy had excited me ever since I read *Joy's Way* in 1988. My dream of meeting him and listening to him came true when I received a brochure announcing his weekend seminar in Albuquerque, New Mexico. I signed up, never imagining how worthwhile this time would be. Dr. Joy has the magic, the sense of humor, and the knowledge which make his lectures spellbinding. Yet it was the private work I did in my hotel room and during group visualization exercises that gave me more priceless tools for personal healing.

An August Saturday morning's Sacred Temple visualization sent my personal power issues into paroxysms. I practically raced out of the conference room and back upstairs to my room during the lunch period. I was crawling inside. Tears were streaming down my cheeks as I sank onto my bed. I wanted to binge, binge, binge! I felt as fat as if I had swallowed a small dirigible. Duality tore me apart. Should I take a walk or not? Eat lunch or not? Rest or not? Cry or write? Obviously, my visualization had agitated me, so I needed to analyze it.

My sacred temple appeared as my two power land animals, the wolf and the cougar, sitting in a "V-shape." Their haunches formed the tip of the "V" while I was situated in the middle of their forms with one hand on each animal. The wolf symbolized my masculine power, and the cougar symbolized my feminine power. They were transmitting their powers to me. They were instructing me to be powerful and to act powerful. They were indicating to me that I must try to work through all my feelings from now on and not escape through bulimia.

Tapping into my power so pictorially was a big shock for me. Side-by-side feelings of being tantalized and repelled sparred within me. I took a walk to avoid thinking.

By the time the evening session began, I was exhausted as well as slightly distracted by my day's revelations. I was mellow and introspective, perhaps acting a bit aloof.

During the break, a woman introduced herself to me and asked if I were a massage therapist. I said, "No, why do you ask?" She said I looked like a massage therapist she knew and respected who had great healing power and sensitivity. This woman added, "You know, you should consider some aspect of the healing profession. You have such a quiet, gentle strength around you." I had been told this many times before, but this night I was especially flattered. The turmoil earlier in the day just evacuated from my head. I floated in elation back up to my hotel room.

The next day, Sunday, the seminar closed with the participants holding hands forming one large circle. Everyone shut their eyes as a cassette tape played a gorgeous, ethereal, female soprano singing notes.

Madame Colorful appeared in my mind's eye, standing in a violet robe. I was kneeling before her. As the singer's voice resounded in a powerful crescendo, Madame Colorful told me to rise. As I did, I transformed into my powerful, mature, feminine goddess. I wore a full-length gown the color of ecru moonlight. It swirled around me like a wispy fog. I stood tall, proud, and competent. I was fueled with strength, beauty, and power! "Assume your position in the world as a powerful woman. It is time for your power to prevail. The bonds to your father and mother are broken. You will now cross the threshold from Terrified Inner Child to Empowered Female!" Madame Colorful mandated.

I felt a surge of energy cleanse me as tears trickled in real life from my eyes. Madame Colorful smiled because she understood my joy and my sense of victory. I felt so happy, so contented, so energized, and so grateful.

Back in my room, I dashed into the bathroom to look at my face. I felt like I must surely have changed. The difference was instantly apparent! My eyes reflected a rich, deep, crystalline sheen. Gazing into my irises, I saw a kaleidoscope of tiny, geometric shapes in various tints of blue. The pores in my face were tightly closed so that my complexion appeared soft and flawless. The hollowness under my cheekbones was gone, and my cheeks were gingerly brushed with a pastel peach hue. I looked twenty years younger. I felt truly alive — body and soul!

That night I was gleaming with energy. It was pouring through and out of me. I lay in bed with the window open, the cool, stiff breeze wafting into the room. I could hear the leaves of the trees along Central Avenue rustling. Turquoise was nestled on my chest amid my hugging arms. The three-quarter moon shined from heaven, occasionally obscured by drifting clouds. I kept remembering my incredible visualization during which I became my Empowered Female. It was so thrilling! But how did Little Suzy feel about the new woman on the scene? I feared she might feel rejected and abandoned. I asked her, "How do you feel about my identifying with this empowering female aspect?"

Bubbling with glee she chirped, "It's about time! I thought you might not ever recognize her. I feel relieved. I know that she won't take you from me. She will enhance your life, and our time together will be of better quality."

My heart was warmed.

I began thinking about Nurturing Adult, the aspect of my personality that I created to be Little Suzy's unconditionally loving parent. The time had come to refine this aspect and to flesh it out. In fact, it was time to split it into two genders: male and female.

For my female parent, I wanted more of the elder, wise woman traits. A mixture of the old Hawaiian tutu, the Native American medicine woman, and the ample, indulgent Black nanny seemed ideal. I wanted her to be gentle, tender, ever-accepting, and always willing to hold and rock my hurting Inner Child. I tossed names around but nothing clicked. Then, the moon slipped from behind a dark cloud and radiated the most intense moonlight I have ever seen or felt. It was clear, direct, and pulsating, as if every moonbeam were being funneled from its source, down a pathway in the sky, through the panes of glass in my window, and into my heart. It was like a laser. I inhaled audibly and integrated the force. Instantly, I knew Little Suzy's nurturing female parent would be called Moon Mother.

Defining my male parent was harder because I couldn't refer to any man who was a complete model of what I wanted. He must love me, guide me, listen to me, and believe in me. He would wear plush, fuzzy sweaters fitting loosely over his broad shoulders and wide chest. He would treat me with respect. We would laugh a lot together. He would put his arms around me, squeeze me, and tell me how dearly he loved me. Like a sturdy, old wall, I could always depend on him to support me. Dr. Kowalski's face popped into my head. Of course! If there were ever a man I would want for a father, it would be Dr. K. Gentle Father was the natural name for Little Suzy's nurturing male parent.

Two more aspects demanded names since they now felt truly real and alive inside me. My competent woman was honest, self-confident, and assertive. She was an astute businesswoman, an impressive public speaker, a talented writer, and a snappy dresser. Her brain worked rapidly, efficiently, and absorbed information easily. Such an upbeat, in-charge woman would be some smart cookie. That's it! Competent Cookie was born.

Now, to name that golden, regal empowered female. Just thinking of her made me feel solid inside — proud to be me. Her energy felt so warm. Without pause Empowered Female Energy, Effie for short, spilled into my mind. Effie it would be!

I was so delighted to have these parts of myself now named and to feel their realness! I could call upon them in conjunction with my power animals, the wolf, the cougar, and the dolphin, whenever I desired their individual characteristics. Implementing them in my daily life was going to be quite beneficial.

Peak Experience #6

THE SWEAT LODGE

For as long as I can remember, I have held deep respect for North American Indian life and spirituality. Their ceremonies hold powerful medicine, and I have long desired to partake in some of them. My daring never matched with my desire until the summer of 1988. It was then that I put forth my wish for a medicine woman to come into my life and teach me some lessons about feminine empowerment.

I had given up hope of receiving such a woman until one day in July, 1989, on the front page of *The Daily Oklahoman* was a feature story about a white shaman in eastern Oklahoma. Woman or man — it didn't seem to matter to me now. Here was a possible answer to my request. Before I knew what I was doing, I was talking to Ross Banister on the phone and had enlisted for his August weekend of gentle initiation.

I hung up the phone wondering if I had lost my mind. I knew nothing about this fellow except for a brief biography and synopsis of his work contained in the newspaper article. The only thing I knew was that my instincts told me I had to go because I was going to be presented with the opportunities to face each of my fears.

So it was, but the sweat lodge ceremony, which provoked my childhood fear of death, particularly altered my life.

When I arrived at Ross's camp late on a Friday afternoon, I was weary from accumulated stress. What was I doing here at the top of a heavily forested mountain, isolated from any help should I need it, parked outside a spartan log cabin with two sentry dogs snapping ferociously outside my car door? As Ross strode out of his cabin, calmed his dogs, and smiled at me, I knew my worries were unfounded. I felt safe and I trusted that feeling.

Over a cup of coffee, Ross and I chatted, and he outlined the agenda for the next forty-four hours. I grew more apprehensive by the minute, and part of me wanted to cancel this entire pilgrimage. The other part of me was eager for this initiation.

Ross is an earnest, courageous warrior, and I respected and enjoyed him from our first moments together. He teaches with a balanced hand, strict yet supportive. Not once did he dispatch me on a mission with, "You will be fine. You can do this." I was conscientiously briefed on each ceremony, told to be back at the cabin whenever I felt finished with my task, and summarily adjourned from the picnic table. My life of self- reliance really came in handy during this weekend!

The sweat lodge ceremony didn't begin until the full moon was high in the sky on Saturday night. By that time, I was fairly high on the stressed-out scale, having had to think about it for about thirty hours! "Throw out this macho stuff! I want my mother!" I complained silently.

At dusk in single file, we hiked up the adjacent hill on a narrow footpath through mild underbrush. To the others, their judicious high stepping was protection against rattle-snakes, but for me, it was poison ivy that threatened. (I hate that plant and contract the rash every time I explore the outdoors.)

Reaching a cleared area atop the knoll, we glimpsed our sweat lodge. It was a turtle-shaped tent made out of willow sticks covered with carpet and a water-resistant hood. East of the sweat lodge was a long, deep fire pit bordered by a low rock wall shaped like a horseshoe with the open end facing the sweat lodge. North of the fire pit was a large, sponge mat covering the mowed stubble. Four humans and two dogs sought asylum on that mat, waiting for darkness.

The wood piled on the rocks in the fire pit crackled and popped and tossed embers into the night air as it burned. We waited and waited. Patience not being my virtue, espe-cially when I'm facing something unpleasant, I finally joked to Ross that if the rocks weren't hot enough soon, he would be minus one sweat person. Handing me the drum and a substantial stick, Ross told me to beat the drum. It was part of the ceremony but surely released a lot of my nervous tension. When I was attuned to the cadence, Ross asked me to hit the drum using my masculine energy. The steady, forceful "boom, boom, boom" connected my energy with the energy of those who performed this ritual eons ago. As we danced around the fire shaking the rattles Ross had

replicated from original Indian ones, I imagined the appari-
tions of proud peoples weaving among us.

The moon climbed higher and higher until Ross announced it was time to enter the sweat lodge. A mass of
anxiety jumped into my heart, and I wanted to burst out
crying. I was petrified, but it was too late now to run.

Ross in the lead, we reverently walked clockwise around
the fire pit, bowed at the entrance of the sweat lodge, and
crawled on all fours inside the structure to our respective
positions. My position was the West. As I situated myself,
I fretted about what might be crawling or living on the
floormat of the lodge. My arms, hands, legs, and feet were
exposed because I was wearing my swim suit. In ten
minutes that worry would be the least of my concerns!

The ceremony inside the sweat lodge consisted of four
series of prayers. The first round of prayers was for ourselves. Before praying, the hot, red rocks were transported
into the cavity in the ground inside the lodge. Ross closed
the flap on the entrance plunging us into the blackest of
blacks. I panicked. This was the color of the blackness
inside my Inner Child. It was tangible. It was heavy. It was
everywhere. My heart lurched so convulsively I thought it
might shoot out of my chest. Calm down. Calm down. You
can handle this, I lied to myself. The moist steam from water
being splashed on the rocks pampered my body. The
delicate aroma of sage tickled my nostrils. I was lulled into
believing this was going to be a piece of cake after all.
Suddenly, fingers of hot, choking steam filled with pungent
sage grabbed me. Little Suzy took over my psyche. I wanted
to scream out for someone to hold my hand and comfort
me, but I was ashamed of appearing cowardly. I felt a panic
attack building, and I was ready to fight and claw my way
out of this inferno.

Then I remembered Ross's earlier instructions that if I
felt too suffocated I could drop my face and inhale the cool
air settled on the floor. I dropped like a meteor, cupped my
hands over my mouth, and drank in a draught of that
sanity-restoring mixture. "Breathe. Keep breathing," I heard

Martha's dictum in my head. If I hadn't been so distraught, I would have had a nice laugh out of that! As it was, I was crying my heart out. Mucus poured from my nose, so I hastily wiped my hands on my thighs and dragged my nose along my right forearm. Nothing was as important as crying. Little Suzy was truly cleaning herself out. When my turn to pray came I sputtered, "E.O.U., send me Light and Love. Love. Love, love, love! Ho!" Ross lifted the flap, and we all scooted toward the opening. Never had I fully appreciated fresh air until that moment. A turtle shell of water was passed around, and a fresh supply of hot rocks was retrieved. Everyone chuckled when I requested that Ross speed up the addressing of the Ancestors and expedite his prayers.

The second round of prayers was for others. My clutching fear of death didn't seize me when the lodge was once more drowned in blackness. I was able to relax, listen to the others, and formulate a sensible prayer of my own.

The third round of prayers was for Light Giveaways, positive things one wants to share with the Universe, and Dark Giveaways, negative things one wants to release. I was fully into this series and didn't even realize Ross had opened the flap at its conclusion. I had my eyes closed and was "at one" with the others. It was a magnificent sensation, and I wanted this round to last longer.

The fourth round of prayers was for expressing gratitude. Strangely, I was flowing with this process until near its conclusion. Like an invisible virus, thoughts of dying invaded my head. My throat and chest tightened as if preparing for the bombardment. But the flap opened, and I saw that sublime moonlight!

Once outside, I drew slowly and lovingly into every fiber of my being the clean, cool, night air. Air! Moonlight! I felt the POWERFUL ME standing there. I stretched my arms heavenward, my crystal clutched in my left hand, a turtle rattle in my right, repeating, "Thank you! Thank you!"

We returned to Ross's cabin, dined on a midnight supper of juicy beef brisket, and parted for our individual campsites, triumphant warriors all! I thought I had reached the pinnacle of pride in myself for this trip, but my ultimate "atta-boy" awaited me the following morning.

After breakfast and a wrap-up, I said my good-byes. As I stepped off the wooden porch onto the pounded dirt, Ross called to me, "You know, it took a lot of guts for you to come up here to a strange man, a wild mountain, and unfamiliar ceremonies."

"Thank you," I uttered and grinned. It did take a lot of guts, and I really appreciated the stroke from the heart of this Caucasian brave they call Strong Hawk.

Peak Experience #7
A DIVORCE HOUSECLEANING

Prior to peak experience #7, I unconsciously observed two anniversaries: September 9, 1989, the ninth anniversary of the signing of my divorce; and September 13, 1989, the ninth anniversary of my departure from Willie and our Alabama home. True to my pattern, it took me awhile to consciously put the puzzle pieces together and to realize what was happening.

For the entire week before September 9, 1989, I experienced my three undeniable, "memories-being-activated" symptoms: (1) slight dizziness (a remnant of my panic attacks), (2) constant hunger and the biting of my contentious Voice, and (3) my "dead pattern." Probable explanations I fished for were my menstrual period, anxiety over a live radio appearance, sorrowful memories emerging as I wrote this book, stress concerning an upcoming weekend trip, and Doug's departure for a business conference.

September 9, 1989, came and went in absolute chaos. It was awful! I wanted to eat everything from the carpet on the floor to the shingles on the roof. I lost one of my contact lenses, and I had never lost one in the whole nine years I had worn them. My mood ricocheted from high enthusiasm to abysmal self-reproach. I couldn't sleep. My brain couldn't hold a thought. Sometimes the thought couldn't even be formulated. I felt so helpless, stupid, and impatient with myself.

The next three days I spent in a listless shroud. My mind felt leaden and rusty. My body felt like someone had siphoned the life out of it.

My Higher Self suggested meditation during which I fell asleep. My unconscious underlined the meaning of the last few days' events.

When I awoke, I dashed to uncover my 1980 calendar, and there were the words on the little square printed with a "Sept. 9" in the upper right hand corner, "Signed divorce papers." So! It was time to tackle this divorce and all the issues dangling from it, such as fear of death and abandonment, loss of my personal identity, and my rage toward men.

As fate would have it, Doug was going to be gone on September 13. Here I was going to have to face more memories alone . . . again. Curses!

Naturally, my first programmed response was to think of a binge/purge. Then I thought, "Why? A binge/purge only means feelings trying to surface. Why not give myself the love and support I truly need instead of forsaking my pain? With Doug gone, it will be an excellent chance to work on residual feelings. I will have the privacy and space to cry, scream, dance — whatever. I can examine the wound, cleanse the remaining pus, channel some blood flow into the injury to speed healing, and then I can bandage it with love, respect, and appreciation. New tissue will regenerate over the opening. The spot may be sore for years to come, but the nasty infection will have been flushed out. Yes! This is a wonderful opportunity for growth!"

Propped up in bed intercepting sadness and anger, I knew a vigorous purgation was necessary. Movement therapy! I opted to dance out my feelings to Rachmaninov's "Piano Concerto No. 3 in D Minor, Op. 30." I gave myself permission to feel whatever feelings tunneled up, and I choreographed my steps as the music resonated within me.

Sorrow was the initial feeling to filter up. My dancing was expansive at this point. Without warning, a barrage of fear rammed me like a sumo wrestler. Despite an avalanche of tears, I kept dancing until the ache in my heart became so unbearable I couldn't move anymore. Clasping my hands over my heart, I pitched forward, knees on the floor and head on the cushion of the recliner. My heart was breaking, and I knew Little Suzy was coming to the forefront. I just let her slip into and fill my body cavity. She began crying out loud, "Please, don't leave me! Please, don't leave me!" Willie's face materialized in my mind. (My Present Adult suspected I was reliving Little Suzy's reaction to Willie's departure around September 6, 1980. I even heard the back door of our new house slam as Willie stormed out.) Like a spillway, Little Suzy's tears overflowed. Swamping my heart was the pain of the loss of all three men in my life, Joe Ben, Daddy, and Willie. It felt like three thundering rivers, each from three different directions, were gushing into me, not out of me. I was again colliding with my core trauma: abandonment. I remained bowed and cried until the feelings shuffled away. All this time the music continued.

My composure restored, I resumed dancing. My movements echoed the choppy, Karate-like rhythm of the concerto. I found myself, feet apart in a wide stance, arms extended skyward, and fist pounding at some invisible enemy. Anger rushed into my body from my feet upward, like an empty glass being filled with water. When the anger reached the top of my head, a ferocious growl escaped my mouth. I screamed and punched the air above me. They were not thin, high, transparent shrieks but possessed a husky, feathered texture like a full-grown lion's roar. They were surging from a tiny place far, far down between my breasts. They had been stuffed from so long ago, and it felt so gratifying to release them. They dried up, and my footwork proceeded.

At the conclusion of "Concerto No. 3 in D Minor," the music swelled and rejoiced. In my mind's eye, I pictured a sunset with its crimsons, violets, and peaches, and I felt so loved. This part of my dance expressed gratitude.

Sensing that my feelings were activated by the movie of my life rolling in my head, I chose Rachmaninov's "Rhapsody on A Theme of Paganini, Op. 43" to complete my purification. I eliminated the loneliness and fear of my post-divorce period, the frenzy of my first stay in Edmond, the disillusionment of Tunisia, and the joy of my current enrichment and healing. I ended, beaming with happiness and hope. What an incomparable victory!

When I emerged from my altered state of consciousness, I found that only thirty minutes had passed. It was 4:45 p.m., but the sun was setting rapidly. Darkness dropped over the beach within fifteen minutes, and I jogged back to the condo feeling wonderfully hungry and wonderfully alive.

20

Final Releasings and Taking Off

BY SUNDAY, NOVEMBER 5, 1989, the turquoise and aquamarine tints had returned to the waters of the Emerald Coast, and I had recouped my lightheartedness. Recounting my peak experiences had filled me with infinite joy, but I still felt unfinished, like the final curtain had yet to fall.

Journal entry, November 6, 1989:

Thinking about:

(1) my relationship with Mother. We were both very vulnerable, each for our own reasons, when my brother died. I understand now why our needs became entangled. At the time, we did the very best we knew how to survive, and I respect our decisions. Our binding happened just as Alice Miller described in Drama Of The Gifted Child. *I understand how I made my conclusions that love is suffocating, that love means sacrificing myself in order to keep others happy, and that love says I have no personal boundaries. I don't regret pushing for answers and demanding to know the why's. The impetus perked from someplace deep within me, and I had no say-so over the impulse. My sanity and freedom were at stake. The important thing for me now is to nurture myself. I am learning what healthy love entails and am chang-*

ing my behavior accordingly. It is time for me to unleash myself from my mother and to go forth into the rest of my life with a strong and loving heart.

(2) my relationship with Doug. Recent, painful self-examination in the last two weeks has shown me that I have been trying to control Doug. I have been imploring him to talk about his feelings, and he is simply not ready to unlock his doors.

It is good that I take care of myself and maintain my "I feel . . ." statements, but I must not then unconsciously expect him to change his behavior to suit me. I must let go. I must value his right to be where he is. I must stop feeling totally responsible for the success of our marriage.

Late entry, November 6, 1989:

This afternoon I found a perfect starfish specimen on the beach! I was out for my daily walk but had no enthusiasm — no zest. I was lost in thought about "letting go" and not paying attention to my present surroundings. Suddenly, my feet stopped moving, and I felt a jolt of energy hit my body. I stood frozen, gazing down at a five-pointed shape. "A starfish! A starfish!" These words reverberated through my head until my mind returned to the present reality. "It IS a starfish! A huge, perfect one!"

"Oh my! I have always wanted to find a starfish on the beach and here it is! What does this mean? Should I take it? Is it a gift to me from the sea, or is it the season of the year for starfish to beach themselves?" I pondered. I felt like a dazzled little child in a pet store. How I wanted to keep this starfish! It seemed like a personal messenger meant for me. I decided to take it.

I rigged up a flimsy support pad of my two flip-flops and a small piece of driftwood and car-

ried my treasure back to the condo. I placed it carefully on a sheet of newspaper and placed it on the deck while I phoned dive shops to inquire as to how to preserve it. "Put it tentacles-side down on a shallow plate in the shade and cover it with formaldehyde," one girl told me. Off I raced to the nearest drugstore only to learn that formaldehyde was a deadly, dangerous chemical not to be handled by a novice.

In a somber frame of mind, I returned to the condo, knowing my starfish would probably inevitably break apart and crumble. I was inundated with sadness.

Night had fallen. I squatted beside my starfish. I examined it and touched its spiny arms. Already tiny chunks of the mosaic covering its tentacles were breaking off. I felt terribly guilty. Would it have lived had I replaced it in its saltwater home? Had I killed this creature for no other reason than to have a trophy? Or was it truly sent to me? Maybe it was sent to me, but not intended for me to confiscate. Maybe POSSESSING it was not the point of the message at all! Maybe just the fact that it was ON the beach — that I was also ON the beach — that I was AT one of my power spots — was the import. "Forgive me, starfish, if I murdered you for nothing," I prayed. I felt very heavy in spirit. Why was I so shook up over this starfish? My gosh! I was even talking to it! I decided to ask my Higher Self to reveal to me in my dreams what the starfish meant.

Journal entry, November 7, 1989:

No memory of dreaming when I awoke to a rainy, gray day. Must be patient. Prepared toast, fruit, and coffee for breakfast and then opened the kitchen blinds and noticed a swaggering breeze tossing the palm tree fronds in the courtyard below my second-story deck.

"Oh my! My starfish!" I choked. I knew I was too late. Sure enough! I opened the sliding glass door, and it felt like a rock dropped from my heart into my abdomen. The starfish was flipped over, two arms were detached, and two others were practically severed. I felt like crying. I picked up the handmade foil plate the starfish had rested upon and scooped up the various pieces of the animal and laid them on the unsubstantial dish. Its tentacles thrashed wildly, and I winced in pain.

Well, what was done was done. Just because the starfish was dismembered didn't mean I loved it any less. Many beautiful souls inhabit physically broken bodies. But one thing was for sure. It wasn't finding a PERFECT specimen per se that was of significance. It was, after all, the fact that it was ON the beach. The message was, "You have asked for direction. I am pointing all around. This area, this beach, is where you need to be because something extraordinarily remarkable will soon befall you." A shiver went down my spine, and I felt uncomfortable for a few seconds.

Still hungry after breakfast, I was tempted to nibble on some Fritos, but knew that one chip would lead to forty, so I gathered up my journals, legal pad, and pencil and decided to work on my book upstairs away from the kitchen.

One foot trudged after the other up the stairs. Like a plane releasing a bomb, I held the stack of notebooks above the bed and let them drop. They hit with a muffled slap. "Boy, am I really enthusiastic," I scoffed sarcastically. I got comfortable in bed, and an eerie series of events unfolded.

Instead of picking up my legal pad, I picked up Lynn Andrews' workbook, Teachings Around The Sacred Wheel. *Why did I reach for this book? I wondered. Thumbing randomly, I stopped at a chapter near the end of the book. My Depriver whined, "You don't have all the materials to do this exercise properly. Forget it. You're tired anyway. Take a nap." Nurturing Adult contradicted, "So what! It won't hurt to read it through to familiarize yourself with it. Do it!"*

As I skimmed the material, Madame Colorful intruded from nowhere, "You are very courageous, but your fears restrain you from living life to the fullest. Your life will always be challenging because your nature is one of constant introspection. The starfish indicates you are at the proper place to receive a special gift of enlightenment."

I conveyed to her that I felt afraid. What if the gift was something sent in a painful package? What if, in my blindness, I couldn't see or hear this special gift?

She smiled and spoke, "There you go again with all your fears. You need not worry. Just trust. It will happen. It will be delivered to you with no effort on your part."

Now I DID feel apprehensive! To my controlling nature, the prospect of spontaneity could sometimes be unsettling.

I was feeling really weary by this time and contemplated a snooze as a prime option. Yet I kept turning the pages of the workbook, absently reading bits and pieces. All at once, I read this sentence, "His eyes, like polished mirrors, are too powerful for you to look into for long." I gasped. There was only one person whose eyes were like that for me — my daddy. I was also struck that this was the first time I had thought about Daddy since arriving in Destin.

I remembered a dream I had exactly one month after he died in which a white-hot, pagan ceremonial mask surrounded by a warm, swirling red mist floated into view. I was terrified. The power emanating from the mask scared me. Suddenly, Daddy's huge brown eyes appeared in the eye holes of the mask and telepathically transferred the information that he was all right and that he loved me.

My concentration returned to the workbook, and I decided to go through this chapter and follow the meditation. I would read a paragraph word by word, ever so slowly, then close my eyes and do my visualizations.

A second sentence almost took my breath away, and I reread it three times, "Sometimes woman must be initiated by man just as man must sometimes be initiated by woman." My body tingled. Something uncommon was happening to me, but all I could do was keep reading.

With a third sentence, my brain activity accelerated. I felt like I was trying to frantically organize some pertinent ideas. Yet I knew if my intellect barged in and tried to figure this out logically, I would lose everything. I just needed to stay with the feelings.

The main character speaks for the first time in this meditation, "My name is Oruncha of Chauritzi. I am a medicine spirit warrior." In today's time, he would be called a doctor. My stars! Daddy was a doctor! Deliberately, I slowed and extended my breaths, trying to calm myself. My heart felt like a sledgehammer. I proceeded according to the guidelines.

The meditation was stupendous as I drew near the end.

The next to the last paragraph begins, "Now look Oruncha in the eyes. Once more, let your eyes hold each other's gaze." I started crying. Tears just uncontrollably streamed up and out. I felt the most loving, gentle, healing energy seep into every cell of my body. Tears kept coming even though I was grounded inside a pervasive place of peace.

Daddy had come back to me through the vehicle of Oruncha. This beach was the one place where Daddy and I enjoyed each other, unshackled from pain and communing without words. How apropos that we should finish our business here! By giving me his blessings to align myself with my personal power, he liberated me from his shadow. I was free! Once and for all, I comprehend on my innermost level how strong and beautiful I am, and that whenever I need courage, love, or direction, I don't have to seek them outside of myself. They are within ME!

It is done. My torment is gone. The wholeness that I had been searching for is manifest. All my life, I have wanted to feel loved with gentleness by my daddy and to achieve separateness from my mother. It feels like I have finally done both!

21

My Train Ride Begins

W HEN I COMPLETED THIS BOOK IN JANUARY, 1990, I crossed over into another new, but not totally unexpected, phase of my life. Picture a ballerina going down memory lane as she thumbs through a rack of hangers holding all the costumes of her career. She delicately and lovingly drops the silky folds of the creamy nightgown she wore in her first role as Clara in "The Nutcracker" to excitedly touch the thick, red taffeta of her current and demanding "Carmen" role. Like her, I felt ready and eager to meet what was ahead of me with all its challenges, joys, and heartaches. Yet at the same time, I was almost paralyzed with fear. Now I had to give my manuscript to my family. Now I had to stand up for what I believed in.

My abandonment issue lunged to the forefront, making me constantly fearful, and my bulimia took a turn for the worse. Yet I handed out manuscripts, slowly but surely, knowing that they would not entirely bring pleasure and might even permanently alter some relationships.

My family was not enthusiastic about my book, so the part of me that wanted their approval felt dirty and ashamed for having written it. Physical ailments besieged me, one after another for five months. A persistent rash on and around my left ear popped up first. Then a nasty cold, sore throat, and cough invaded my head, neck, and chest for a month. Though spring was only three weeks away and outside temperatures were mild, I was constantly shivering and my hands and feet felt like ice. Next, my right jaw filled with a piercing pain which later shot out of the bone and fanned into the right side of my face. It was as if sharp claws were trying to rip my cheek and eye out. The most debilitating symptom, by far, was the paralyzing ache in my legs. By mid-June, it was an effort for me to walk. In addition, I was sleeping about eighteen hours a day and crying uncontrollably. I knew I was in the midst of a depression, and though I was impatient to have my health back, I knew these symptoms would have to run their course. The Voice wanted one last hurrah and would not surrender without a show of force.

What surprised me most during these months was the constant availability of my new, strong, healthy attitudes. Whenever the teeter-totter hit the ground on the Voice's side, my Nurturing Adult restored the balance with a positive thought. I had more self-confidence and deeper self-love than ever before. I found a joy in living I had never had because I appreciated the present moment and all the beauty within it. I was so incredibly grateful for who I was and what I had been through. I did not want to be anyone else in this whole, wide world! By finishing my book, I took another step in disassociating myself from my unconscious identification with death. I challenged the mental contract that said I didn't deserve to be alive.

Every therapy and every tool I used, coupled with perseverance, brought me to this place of freedom. I sorted and picked from a wide variety of options available along the way. My healing choices might not be suitable to someone else. The important thing I want to pass on is that, indeed, the journey to recovery is very individual. Each of us must mend according to our own schedule and employing what works for us. Being patient with myself when I failed or when I felt I wasn't perfect was the toughest exercise to practice. Yet by patting myself on the back for every TINY success, I amassed a cornucopia of accomplishments at the end of each day. Don't let anyone tell you small things don't count because in the process of congratulating myself, I ended up with the biggest prize of all. I became my own best friend. You, too, have a best friend inside of you. I wish you Love and Light in discovering him or her.

It is said that life is the train ride, not the arrival at the depot. I feel like my train ride has just begun, and I want to see all the scenery and meet all the people I can. I am so excited!

Epilogue

I remain in therapy strengthening my self-image, incor-
porating a broader knowledge of self-nurturing behaviors,
and reaffirming my right to life. I do not have complete
abstinence yet but continue working toward it each day. I
am eating three nutritious meals a day with sweets, when
and if I want them, although sometimes I still become a bit
too conscientious about what I eat overall.

As for the issue of sexual abuse, I have ruled out the
possibility that I was a victim. My mother emphatically
states that neither she nor I was ever raped. She asked me
to remove all references to possible rape or sexual abuse
from the final manuscript. I declined because it was the
very consideration of the sexual abuse subject which
forced me to quit running from myself and to confront the
roots of my own bodily shame, my fearful and hostile
attitudes toward men, and my persistent bulimia. To compromise what I felt was vital to the unfolding of my story
would have been untrue to my Self. If there is one thing I
have learned from this trek into myself, it is that I must trust
and be true to my Self.

My sexual block stemmed from my rejection of my
feelings. As long as I did not feel feelings, I felt safe, and
safety became the top priority in my life after my brother's
death. I clamped down on that life force which provided

me my spontaneity, my joy, my creativity — my enthusiasm for living.

Now I realize that entering puberty meant more than becoming a woman to me. It marked my entrance into adulthood, and adulthood meant accepting countless responsibilities, all of which I viewed as somber and burdensome. I saw no FUN in being an adult. I was already trying to carry the guilt, the rage, and the sadness of my whole family. With puberty, I would have to carry the added load of my own personal life as well. I felt swamped with inadequacy and ran from the thought of growing up. I shut down some more and dissociated from all sexual feelings so as to reinforce my safety.

Reconnecting with myself and the world is at times arduous and at times exhilarating. It is always risky. At least, now I know it is not necessarily unsafe.

I can sincerely say I love my parents, and I honor them for who and what they were and are. I have emerged from my grieving process with them and have let them go. They loved me and provided for me, and I am grateful for them.

Thank you, Mother, for your generosity, your willingness to laugh, and for the healthy way you took care of your body during your pregnancy with me.

Thank you, Daddy, for instilling in me the love of reading and a devotion to Nature.

Sources of Inspiration

Here is a list of books that were invaluable to me on my journey.

Koller, Alice., *An Unknown Woman*, New York: Holt, Reinhart and Winston, 1981.

Sandbek, Terence J., Ph.D., *The Deadly Diet, Recovering From Anorexia & Bulimia*, Oakland, CA: New Harbinger Publications, Inc., 1986.

Whitfield, Charles L., *Healing The Child Within*, Deerfield Beach, FL: Health Communications, Inc., 1987.

Gawain, Shakti., *Living In The Light*, San Rafael, CA: Whatever Publishing, Inc., 1986.

Levine, Stephen., *A Gradual Awakening*, Garden City, NY: Anchor Books ed., Anchor Press/Doubleday, 1979.

Zukav, Gary., *The Seat Of The Soul*, New York: Simon & Schuster, Inc., 1989.

Lerner, Harriet Goldhor, Ph.D., *The Dance Of Intimacy*, New York: Harper & Row, Publishers, Inc., 1989.

O'Neill, Cherry Boone., *Starving For Attention*, New York: The Continuum Publishing Company, 1982.

Jung, Carl., *Memories, Dreams, Reflections*, New York: Pantheon Books, 1963.

Boskind-White, Marlene, Ph.D., and, William C. White, Jr., Ph.D. , *Bulimarexia, The Binge/Purge Cycle*, New York: W. W. Norton & Company, Inc., 1983.

Levenkron, Steven., *Treating And Overcoming Anorexia Nervosa*, New York: Warner Books, Inc., 1982.

Norwood, Robin., *Women Who Love Too Much*, New York: St. Martin's Press, Inc., 1985.

Fossum, Merle A., and Marilyn J. Mason., *Facing Shame, Families In Recovery*, New York: W. W. Norton & Company, Inc., 1986.

Shainess, Natalie, M.D., *Sweet Suffering*, New York: Pocket Books, div. Simon & Schuster, Inc., 1984.

Friday, Nancy., *My Mother, Myself, The Daughter's Search For Identity*, New York: Delacorte Press, 1977.

Joy, W. Brugh, M.D., *Joy's Way*, Los Angeles: J. P. Tarcher, Inc., 1979.

Baldwin, Martha, M.S.S.W., *Nurture Yourself To Success*, Moore Haven, FL: Rainbow Books, 1987.

Miller, Alice., *Drama Of The Gifted Child*, Frankfurt A/M: Suhrkamp Verlag (original German), 1979; Basic (reprint), 1990.

Bower, Sharon A., and Gordon H. Bower., *Asserting Yourself*, Reading, MA: Addison-Wesley Publishing Company, Inc., 1976.

Bradshaw, John., *Healing The Shame That Binds You*, Deerfield Beach, FL: Health Communications, Inc., 1988.

Leonard, Linda., *The Wounded Woman*, Boston: Shambhala Publications, Inc., 1982.

Axline, Virginia., *Dibs In Search Of Self*, Boston: Houghton Mifflin, 1964.

Orbach, Susie., *Fat Is A Feminist Issue*, New York: Paddington Press, Ltd., 1978.

Roth, Geneen., *Feeding The Hungry Heart, The Experience Of Compulsive Eating*, Indianapolis: Bobbs-Merrill Co., Inc., 1982.

Roth, Geneen., *Breaking Free From Compulsive Eating*, New York: Macmillan, 1985.

Fields, Suzanne., *Like Father, Like Daughter: How Father Shapes The Woman His Daughter Becomes*, Boston: Little, Brown & Co., 1983.

Viorst, Judith., *Necessary Losses*, New York: Ballantine Books, div. Random House, Inc., 1986.

Mariechild, Diane., *The Inner Dance*, Freedom, CA: The Crossing Press, 1987.

Hay, Louise., *Heal Your Body*, Santa Monica, CA: Hay House, 1982.

Gravitz, Herbert L., and Julie D. Bowden., *Guide To Recovery, A Book For Adult Children of Alcoholics*, Holmes Beach, FL: Learning Publications, Inc., 1985.

Mowat, Farley., *Never Cry Wolf*, Boston: Little, Brown and Company, 1963.

Rubin, Jerry., *Growing (Up) At 37*, New York: M. Evans, 1976.

Carson, Richard., *Taming Your Gremlin*, New York: Harper & Row, Publishers, Inc., 1983.

Pierce, Joseph Chilton., *Magical Child*, New York: E. P. Dutton, 1977.

Jung, Carl., *Man And His Symbols*, New York: Dell Publishing Co., 1964.

MacLaine, Shirley., *Out On A Limb*, New York: Bantam Books, 1983.

Leonard, Jim, and Phil Laut., *Rebirthing, The Science Of Enjoying All Of Your Life*, Cincinnati: Trinity Publications, 1983.

Capacchione, Lucia, M.A., *The Power Of Your Other Hand*, North Hollywood, CA: Newcastle Publishing Co., Inc., 1988.

Edwards, Betty., *Drawing On The Right Side Of The Brain*, Los Angeles: J. P. Tarcher, Inc., 1979.

Hyatt, Carole, and Linda Gottlieb., *When Smart People Fail*, New York: Simon & Schuster, Inc., 1987.

Bruch, Hilde, M.D., *The Golden Cage, The Enigma Of Anorexia Nervosa*, Cambridge, MA: Harvard University Press, 1978.

Chernin, Kim., *The Hungry Self, Women, Eating, & Identity*, New York: Times Books, 1985.

Rubin, Theodore Isaac., *The Angry Book*, New York: Collier, 1969.

Dychtwald, Ken., *Body-Mind*, New York: J. P. Tarcher, 1986.

Peck, M. Scott, M.D., *The Road Less Travelled*, New York: Simon & Schuster, Inc., 1978.

Gaylin, Willard, M.D., *Feelings*, New York: Harper & Row, 1979.

Andrews, Lynn V., *Medicine Woman*, New York: Harper & Row, Publishers, Inc., 1981.

Andrews, Lynn V., *Teachings Around The Sacred Wheel*, San Francisco: Harper & Row, Publishers, 1990.

Jarvis-Kirkendall, Carol, and Jeffery Kirkendall., *Without Consent, How To Overcome Childhood Sexual Abuse*, Scottsdale, AZ: Swan Press, Inc., 1989.

Woititz, Janet G., *Healing Your Sexual Self*, Deerfield Beach, FL: Health Communications, Inc., 1989.

About the Author

When Susan Merkel was a toddler, her eight-year-old brother drowned. Her parents, whose marriage was strained prior to the event, reacted by withdrawing from each other and their two daughters. Two-and-a-half-year-old Susan perceived the loss of their affection as a personal rejection. To protect herself from further hurt, she came to trust only herself, denying that she needed anything from her parents or everyone else.

Suffering from a syndrome known as survivor guilt, she had a childhood filled with the fear of being abandoned or physically hurt. As she passed into puberty, however, she looked for ways to stunt the growth of her body — a form of self-mutilation. She hated being female, thinking that a more masculine appearance would ease the pain thrust upon her parents by the loss of their son. Anorexic but ultimately betrayed by her body, she believed that only with her intelligence could she give them pleasure. Plunging into academics, she became an honor student.

At age twenty, she married her first love, hoping to find in marriage an acceptance that had eluded her in the home of her parents. Within two years she was bulimic, struggling with events which she saw as a succession of personal failures. For ten years, her husband lived with her disorder. Finally, he realized that he would never understand and could no longer forgive her self-destructive behavior. He asked for a divorce. She was thirty-two and panic stricken.

Three years later, in 1983, Susan married a compassionate man who knew about her illness and loved her in spite of it. He vowed to help her, and the healing process began.

It wasn't easy. Alcohol abuse became a regular occurrence, and she became further entrapped in the helplessness and denial epitomized in her bulimia. As she struggled to free herself from her unconscious covenant with death, she entered college. She opened herself to therapy and developed friendships. Majoring in psychology, she took a leadership position at the college and in the community. She graduated *summa cum laude*. And she walked on the road of recovery.

Her biography, *Certifiably Bulimic*, is a chronicle of the incredible pain and the magnificent gifts which have come to Susan Merkel. She says, "My book is my expression of gratitude to the Universe and my offering of hope to others trapped in despair and addictions."

To order additional copies of *Certifiably Bulimic*
by Susan Merkel,
send $12.95 plus $3.00 shipping/handling
for each copy ordered to:
Distinctive Publishing Corp.
P.O. Box 17868
Plantation FL 33318-7868

Quantity discounts are also available from the publisher.